MICROSOFT
®

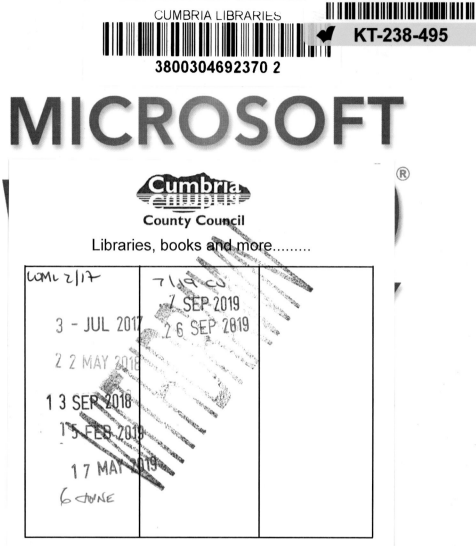

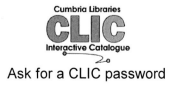

Publisher and Creative Director: Nick Wells
Project Editor: Polly Prior
Art Director: Mike Spender
Layout Design: Jane Ashley
Digital Design and Production: Chris Herbert
Screenshots: James Stables, Matthew Hanson
Copy Editor: Anna Groves
Proofreader: Amanda Crook
Indexer: Helen Snaith

Special Thanks: Matthew Hanson, Catherine Taylor, Jérémie Lebaudy

FLAME TREE PUBLISHING
6 Melbray Mews
Fulham, London SW6 3NS
United Kingdom

www.flametreepublishing.com

This edition first published 2017

17 19 21 20 18
1 3 5 7 9 10 8 6 4 2

ISBN 978-1-78664-169-4

© 2017 Flame Tree Publishing

A CIP record for this book is available from the British Library upon request.

Printed in China

Image Credits:

Screenshots courtesy of Flame Tree Publishing Ltd/James Stables or Matthew Hanson and © the respective software organisation.

Microsoft product shots (including lifestyle shots) used with permission from Microsoft, © 2016 Microsoft Corporation.

Non-Microsoft product shots courtesy the following: © ASUSTeK Computer Inc. 18t; © Intel Corporation 26; © 1996-2016 NETGEAR® 124; © 2016 Belkin International,Inc. 125b; © PixLink 126; Copyright © Canon (UK) Ltd 2016 184; Copyright © 2014 Western Digital Technologies, Inc. 229.

All other non-screenshot pictures: courtesy Shutterstock.com and the following suppliers: Oleksiy Mark 3, 5b & 98–99; Stanislaw Mikulski 4 & 14–15; Rawpixel.com 5c & 76–77; wrangler 5t & 32–33; asharkyu 6t & 122–23; Mybona 6b & 162–63; Dragon Images 7t & 192–93; You can more 7b & 226–27; michaeljung 8; wavebreakmedia 10b; Monkey Business Images 11; Georgejmclittle 12; valdis torms 13; Anteromite 17; Pressmaster 23; dotshock 25t; omihay 35; serato 65b; Ditty_about_summer 73b; RoSonic 90; Twin Design 91t; Babii Nadiia 125c; Oris Arisara 125t; Sebastien Coell 174t; Blend Images 178; Syda Productions 180.

MICROSOFT WINDOWS 10® MADE EASY

JAMES STABLES

FLAME TREE
PUBLISHING

CONTENTS

We know Windows 10 is the latest version in Microsoft's ubiquitous line-up of operating systems, but what's changed? What are the differences between the versions, what's happened in the latest update and, most importantly, how do you get involved? Well, this chapter helps you to get the right version and install it fuss-free and safely.

In this chapter we show you how to get started, from creating a user account and logging in securely to searching, snapping windows and finding your files. In other words, everything you need to start using Windows 10 confidently and proficiently.

Windows isn't just about PCs any more. Our personal devices now come in all shapes and sizes, and Windows 10 is the first operating system to work across your phone, tablet and PC. We discover how Windows unifies all these devices as well as learning about the best universal apps to keep everything running smoothly. Windows tablet and hybrid users can also find out how to make the most of touch-screen gestures.

Every top operating system has an app store and Windows 10 is no different. The Windows Store is jammed with ready-to-download apps. This chapter covers browsing, downloading and managing apps, as well as making sure you download safe and secure names. From dealing with payments and finding the apps you'll love, to bringing your Start menu to life with Live Tiles, everything you need is here.

GET CONNECTED

Windows 10 is specifically designed to hook into the Internet and once you're connected, your PC will be given a new lease of life. This chapter deals with getting online and connecting your PC, getting those essential emails and even starting out in social networking. Windows 10 is a potent force indeed, and with it's full potential on your side you'll find everything you do on your PC considerably enhanced.

GET ORGANIZED

Making your life easier is one of the pillars of Windows 10, and it can help you take control of your digital life. From organizing your time via calendars to getting on top of email, Windows 10 has all the built-in apps you need to get started – no downloads required. We also guide you through using OneDrive, Windows 10's huge online storage feature that lets you access your files from anywhere.

LOOK, WATCH AND PLAY

Windows 10 isn't just about work, work and more work. It also has superb facilities for downloading and playing the latest music, TV shows and movies with the ability to stream, buy and rent. We guide you around the all-new Groove Music app as well as showing you how to kick back and relax. Gaming is a huge part of Windows 10, and any user with an Xbox or a passing interest in games shouldn't miss this essential chapter.

MAINTAIN

Your PC is a fine-tuned machine, and like any engine it needs some maintenance to make sure it runs smoothly. This chapter is dedicated to keeping your PC in top working order, making sure it runs quickly and efficiently. If you do encounter problems, then this is the chapter that will help you sort them out fast.

INTRODUCTION

Jumping into any new operating system can be tough, and everyone needs a little help to guide them. That's where *Windows 10 Made Easy* comes in. Designed as an essential companion, it's there when you need it to help you through your entire Windows 10 journey, from that uncertain first hour to those dicey moments when things go wrong.

EASY TO UNDERSTAND

Not everyone's a PC expert and no-one likes a know-all talking in tech speak and jargon. *Windows 10 Made Easy* aims to cut through all that, breaking down complicated aspects of even the toughest parts of Windows 10 and helping anyone to master them quickly, easily and safely.

USE WINDOWS 10 WITH CONFIDENCE

The aim of *Windows 10 Made Easy* is to help you use your Windows 10 PC with confidence. Many people are too scared about breaking their PC to try new things, but in reality, that's very hard to do. This book is designed to show you what Windows 10 is capable of and give you ideas to explore – secure in the knowledge that your PC is safe and protected.

Above All the screenshots in this book have been chosen to highlight or further illustrate what is being said in the text.

CLEAR SCREENSHOTS

We've spent time examining every aspect of the operating system, and we've tested and demonstrated and taken screenshots along the way. They're not just there for decoration; they're designed to show you where options are and how to get there, helping you really start to learn this brilliant operating system.

WRITTEN BY EXPERTS

Windows 10 Made Easy is the result of a decade of experience writing guides and tutorials about the Windows operating system. The author's years of writing and editing magazines, books, periodicals and even instructional videos on Windows XP, Vista, 7 and more recently Windows 8 means *Windows 10 Made Easy* is the only resource you'll need.

Above: Microsoft has created an operating system that truly works across many devices.

DESIGNED FOR EVERYONE

Not only is *Windows 10 Made Easy* designed for every type of user – from beginner to advanced – it's also written for every type of device. Windows 10 has not only arrived for PCs but also for phones and tablets. This book is written with all types of devices in mind, whether you're using Windows 10 on your old-school desktop or brand-new hybrid PC.

NEW IDEAS

If you're not using your PC to its fullest capabilities, you're missing out on huge enhancements to your hobbies and everyday life. If you haven't heard of music streaming, then you haven't discovered the power of having 30 million songs at your fingertips. If you haven't used cloud computing, you haven't harnessed the power of having your files anywhere and haven't got the peace of mind of knowing that your precious documents and memories are safe from disaster.

Windows 10 Made Easy enables you to do all these things and so much more, and this guide is your key to unlocking a world of new ideas and possibilities.

EIGHT IN-DEPTH CHAPTERS

Whether you're struggling to open Windows 10 for the first time or fed up with only having a basic knowledge of using your PC, this guide is for you. We take you from the basics of the system to some of its best and most hidden features. You'll discover that Windows 10 is the perfect OS, whether you're an absolute beginner or a seasoned IT professional.

The first chapter introduces all the changes in Windows 10, and explains why this operating system is built for a world full of devices. We show you how to take advantage of the latest features, and which version of Windows as well as which type of device is best for you.

Next, we take you through the basics of the OS, and what to do in the first hour of turning on your PC. By the end of it, you'll be securely set up and can get on with using your PC with the ultimate peace of mind. The next two chapters introduce Windows 10 on mobile devices before we dive into the exciting world of apps.

Then we spend some time getting connected and managing the digital deluge of our connected lives with the built-in tools in Windows 10, before we explain in detail how to use your PC for fun rather than for work.

Finally we have a whole chapter dedicated to keeping your PC running properly, and how to overcome problems. From fixing a slow and stuttering PC to recovering from crashes without losing your files, *Windows 10 Made Easy* arms you with the knowledge of why problems arise, and walks you through the tools that not only solve them, but also prevent them from happening in the first place.

Hot Tips

As we guide you on your voyage of Windows 10 discovery, we've also included some hot tips for getting even more out of your Windows 10 experience. From quick shortcuts to hacks for power users, these tips will turn you into a true Windows expert.

JARGON BUSTING

Technology is all too often packed with terminology that can seem like another language to the uninitiated. Unfortunately much of it is unavoidable, and understanding the terminology is an essential part of getting the most from your system. That's why we've taken the opportunity to explain the most important terms, so you can boost your understanding of your PC.

STEP-BY-STEP GUIDES

Each section of this guide features easy-to-follow, step-by-step guides, which walk you through every aspect of Windows 10's numerous features. *Windows 10 Made Easy* offers clear and concise explanations for every part of the operating system with simple walkthroughs when things get difficult, to help you every step of the way.

INTRODUCING WINDOWS 10

A MAJOR MOVE FORWARD

Windows 10 is the latest in Microsoft's historic line of operating systems, and it represents a major shift in the way our devices function. It works across phones, tablets and computers, from massive desktops to pocket-size handhelds. With regular updates and new features landing all the time, the days of sticking with one operating system for years could be over.

WHAT IS WINDOWS 10?

Windows 10 is the latest and greatest version of Microsoft's operating system, released in the same year that it turned 30 years old. While computers have changed almost beyond recognition since 1985, the role of the operating system hasn't.

What Happened to Windows 9?

Now let's get something straight: you didn't miss Windows 9. One theory as to exactly why Microsoft skipped the number 9 is given opposite, but Windows 10 is here. Windows is still by far the world's most popular operating system and since its release in 2015, Windows 10 has

been installed on hundreds of millions of PCs across the globe, although it is no longer offered as a free upgrade.

What Is an Operating System?

The Windows operating system (OS) is responsible for everything your PC does, and without it programs wouldn't be able to run, you wouldn't be able to access the Internet or do any of the incredible things your PC makes possible.

Did You Know?

Windows 95 and 98 were codenamed 'Windows 9x' in the code of Windows, which would cause a massive headache for developers making new software. So to stop huge confusion, Microsoft skipped the number 9 altogether.

That's why it's so important to use your OS to its fullest potential. Whether it's getting more done, having more fun or simply making your PC work better, this is all done through the OS. If you know Windows, then you know your PC inside out.

Without an operating system, the bundle of wires, microchips and circuitry that make up your PC would be useless. All that technology is designed to run one program – the operating system – which in turn acts as the environment for all the programs you use.

The Modern OS

If you run any program, app or game it lives within the OS. Installing something means adding it into the operating system. Every connected gadget you can imagine has an operating system, from your shiny new phone to your thermostat. All these gadgets need an operating system to work.

Back in the old days, PCs were made up of a tower, screen, keyboard and mouse, and even when laptops rose to prominence, the idea was still the same. Devices such as the iPhone and iPad have changed the way we use PCs. However, the role of the operating system has remained exactly the same.

Below: The operating system is the bridge between the hardware and you.

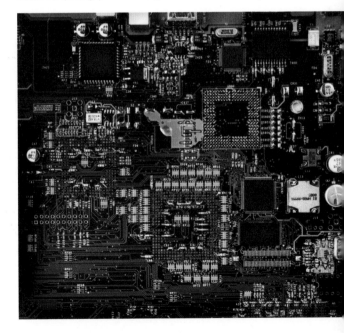

> ## Did You Know?
> The average British household owns
> 7.8 Internet-connected devices.

Above: Laptops and tablets have taken over from the 'netbook'.

THE CHANGING FACE OF COMPUTING

In the main, desktop PCs are now all but dead and, while laptops are still the most popular way of using Windows, tablets and phones are revolutionizing technology. And the things we use tech for are changing, too. Hybrids, which are tablets and laptops all in one, are gaining popularity and super-sized phones have gone from a wacky luxury to the norm.

Above: PCs have got a lot smaller over the years.

Most people now have more than one PC, and when you count your smartphone and tablet, there can be more than five in your personal possession.

Beyond the PC
Windows 10 is the first version of Windows to break out from the PC and put one OS on your desktop, laptop, tablet and phone. Even the Xbox is involved, and it's now able to run Windows apps and sync information between devices.

What does that mean? Well, no more emailing yourself files. No more complaining that the thing you need is on another PC. Or that you don't have Word or a specific app on your device. It's a giant step towards a totally unified experience, and the big difference from the promises of Windows 8 is that this time it's seamless.

DIFFERENCES FROM WINDOWS 8

There's a rule with Windows versions: every other release is great. The rule has been repeated for nearly 20 years: Windows 95 good, Windows 98 not so much; Windows XP was loved, while Vista was hated; Windows 7 was a raging success, and now Windows 10 fixes the shortcomings of Windows 8.

Every time Windows is updated, you get a whole new set of features, and Windows 10 is no different. While visually it's a refinement of the new-look Windows heralded by Windows 8, there are many improvements.

Above: The Start menu is back and completely overhauled.

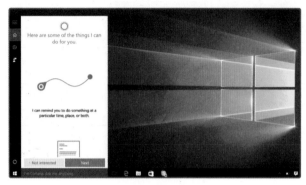

Above: Windows 10 heralds a host of new features.

Above: Internet Explorer is dead and Windows Edge is the new browser.

Above: The Settings menu is a touch-screen friendly way of controlling your PC.

The most notable difference is the Start menu, which returns by popular demand after losing its traditional place on the Windows 8 home screen. Then there's Cortana, a voice assistant brought over from Windows Phone, which listens out for your commands, leaving you free from the mouse and keyboard.

Windows 10 New Features

- Start menu
- Windows Hello
- Windows Passport
- Ability to use your PC like a tablet
- Better cloud-storage integration
- Different experiences for tablet and desktop
- New window snapping
- New unified music and video apps
- Updates to all apps
- Brand new Internet browser called Edge
- In-page doodles anywhere
- Cortana
- New family safety controls
- Xbox integration
- New photos app

WINDOWS 10 VERSIONS EXPLAINED

Windows 10 doesn't just come in one flavour. There are different versions for home users, businesses and even a new version for phones and tablets. Each version has its own features, and can have some startling omissions. Let's take you through the Windows 10 family.

WINDOWS 10 HOME

Windows 10 Home is the everyday edition that will serve most users perfectly comfortably. You'll find this version pre-installed on most PCs found in stores and online.

What Do You Get?

Windows 10 Home has all the main features: the ability to run any Windows application, access to the Windows Store and the full use of the Start screen and traditional desktop. There are applications for watching films and viewing photos, running email and calendars, as well as built-in security protection. You also get full access to all the extra cloud services, such as OneDrive.

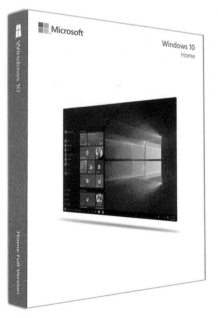

Windows 10 Anniversary Update

A year after the launch of Windows 10, Microsoft celebrated by releasing the free Windows 10 Anniversary Update. This is much more than a standard Windows update, as it brings a range of new features and improvements, such as better integration with smartphones, a more powerful Cortana and an improved Start menu.

How Do You Get It?

The usual way to get Windows is to either buy a new PC or grab an off-the-shelf copy, and that's not changed for Windows 10. Microsoft determined upgrades would be available free of charge to users of Windows 7 or 8 in the first year of Windows 10's release, but since then you'll need to pay for the upgrade. See pages 28–31 for full details on how to get started.

WINDOWS 10 PROFESSIONAL

The Professional edition of Windows 10 is aimed at business users who need more features than people who use their PCs for ordinary home-computing tasks.

What Do You Get?

In Windows 10 Professional you get everything from the Home edition, with added business features designed to boost security and help deal with multiple employees.

Above: The Professional edition is aimed at small to medium-sized businesses.

The first is BitLocker, which is an advanced encryption feature for your PC, which keeps all your files behind an impenetrable wall, in case your laptop or tablet is lost or stolen.

You can also take advantage of Remote Desktop tools, so users can remotely connect to their PC, making files and folders accessible from anywhere in the world. There's also group policy management, so you can manage the PC settings of employees' machines.

How Do You Get It?

Windows 10 Professional was available as a free download for Windows 7 and Windows 8 Professional owners in the first year, but now you'll need to buy Windows 10 Professional off the shelf or as a download.

WINDOWS 10 ENTERPRISE

Windows 10 Enterprise is mainly for large organizations such as schools or businesses, typically with 20 or more people.

What Do You Get?

Really advanced features such as the ability to lock down the entire system or restrict parts of the operating system. Only those looking after large organizations and business data need worry about Enterprise.

How Do You Get It?

To get Windows 10 Enterprise you need to buy a licence that covers the size of your business and every computer. It's a complex task, but you can learn more at www.microsoft.com/licensing

Did You Know?

If you have Windows 10 Home you can pay to upgrade to a Professional edition, which is better for business users.

WINDOWS 10 MOBILE

Windows 10 Mobile will run on smartphones and low-powered tablets, just as the Windows RT version used to.

What Do You Get?

It's designed to run the same apps as the Home and Professional versions but on smaller devices, so you get a unified experience between your laptop and smartphone.

Windows 10 Mobile devices tend to operate at lower power than traditional PCs, so you get dramatically better battery life. It's designed to work with your Windows 10 PC, so both Action Centres will sync up and you will receive unified notifications. As well as universal apps, you will also get versions of Word, Excel and PowerPoint.

Above: Windows 10 Mobile is designed to run on smartphones.

How Do You Get It?

You won't be able to go out there and buy Windows 10 Mobile, but many Lumia phones are now able to get the upgrade. Microsoft confirmed upgrades to the Lumia 1520, Lumia 930, Lumia 640, Lumia 640XL, Lumia 730, Lumia 735, Lumia 830, Lumia 532, Lumia 535, Lumia 540, Lumia 635 (1GB RAM), Lumia 636 (1GB RAM), Lumia 638 (1GB RAM), Lumia 430 and Lumia 435.

WINDOWS 10 EDUCATION

Windows 10 Education is designed to meet the needs of schools – staff, administrators, teachers and students.

What Do You Get?

It very much resembles Windows 10 Enterprise, in that it's designed to be rolled out across institutions, rather than on individual PCs. In terms of features, you get everything. Windows

10 Education benefits from every single feature, to help students learn and administrators manage potentially thousands of networked PCs.

How Do You Get It?

This edition will be available through academic Volume Licensing, and there will be paths for schools and students using Windows 10 Home and Windows 10 Professional devices to upgrade to Windows 10 Education.

Above: Windows 10 now offers the same experience across a host of computer and device sizes.

HARDWARE REQUIREMENTS FOR WINDOWS 10

There is a handy tool on the Microsoft website that can analyse your system and check your hardware. When you go to upgrade to Windows 10 it will automatically check your system using the Windows 10 Upgrade Advisor.

Using the tool on the Windows website is an easy way, but if you don't have access to the Internet, or need an at-a-glance list, here's everything you need.

Hot Tip

Windows 10 is actually less demanding on your PC's hardware than its predecessor Windows 8, so if you have a last-generation system, you should be fine to upgrade.

Processor

To run properly, your PC will need a 1.0GHz (gigahertz) or faster processor. However, it's recommended that your computer's processor should be a dual-core model. Most PCs from the last six years will have the required processor, but if yours is older, it would be unwise to upgrade.

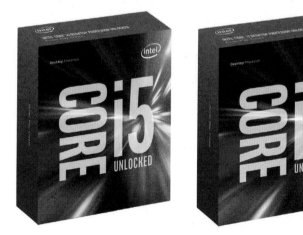

Above: The processor is the brains of your PC. It should be at least dual-core – but can be quad-core, like Intel's enthusiast-class Core i7-6700K and Core i5-6600K.

RAM

Since the Windows 10 Anniversary Update, you will now need 2GB (gigabyte) of RAM to run Windows, but at least 4GB is advisable. You can check the amount of RAM in Windows 7 by right-clicking Computer in the Start menu and choosing Properties or by searching 'System' in Windows 8.

You can use the Start menu almost entirely using the keyboard. Hit Windows key and you can then use the search feature and the arrow keys to navigate it without a mouse.

Hard Disk Space

Installing Windows 10 will take up between 16GB and 32GB of hard disk space depending on the version, and you can check how much you have left by right-clicking your C: drive in Computer/My Computer (in Windows 7) and choosing Properties. In Windows 8 right-click your C: drive in File Explorer. If you have less than 50GB of free space, it's advisable to have a clear out.

Graphics Card

This is where things get more complicated. Windows 10 requires a Microsoft DirectX 9 graphics device, which should be standard on any PC from the last six years or more. If your PC is older, make sure you take the online test.

Touch Screen

If you want to start using Windows 10 to its full touch-screen potential, but don't own a touch-screen laptop, there are options. If you're upgrading an old laptop, you're pretty much stuck, but there are external touch-screen monitors available, which can breathe new life into a desktop PC.

Above: More and more PCs allow for touch-screen control.

GETTING WINDOWS 10

Unlike in the first year of its release, Windows 10 is no longer a free upgrade. But it's still easy to get up and running on any PC. Here we take you through the various ways to upgrade, as well as show you how you can still get Windows 10 for free.

HOW TO UPGRADE YOUR PC TO WINDOWS 10

The process of upgrading your PC to Windows 10 should be fairly simple, and only takes around an hour. However, make sure your precious files and photos are backed up properly first. Then follow the steps below.

Choose What Version of Windows 10 You Want

We've previously outlined the different versions of Windows 10, so now you'll need to decide which one best suits your needs. You also need to bear in mind the different prices, as Windows 10 Home costs £100/$120, while Windows 10 Pro costs £190/$200.

Download the Upgrade Tool

To upgrade to Windows 10, you'll need to open up a web browser and go to www.microsoft.com/en-us/software-download/windows10. You want to install the Windows 10 download tool, so under where it says 'Looking to install Windows 10 on your PC?' click the blue 'Download tool now' button.

Below: The Windows 10 download tool will take you through the process of installing Windows 10.

Use the Download Tool

Once the download tool has downloaded, click on it and it will take you through the process of installing Windows 10. The new operating system will be downloaded in the background. This will take a while and will be held until you tell your PC you're ready to take the plunge and upgrade. The icon will stay in the tray waiting for you.

Above: When you've registered you can download the OS upgrade.

Install

When downloaded you can choose whether you upgrade immediately or schedule it for later, which is a neat touch, so everything can be completed while you sleep. Upgrading generally takes about 40 minutes, but it can be a couple of hours. Your PC will restart a few times during that period.

Everything in Its Right Place

If you're upgrading your PC, your system should wake up with everything as you left it, just within the new operating system. Everything from the location of your files to your favourite desktop wallpaper should remain as was.

> ### Hot Tip
> Right-click the button at the far right of the taskbar and choose 'Peek at desktop'. Hover your mouse over to look at the desktop free of windows and clutter. Your windows will return as you move the mouse away.

HOW TO STILL GET WINDOWS 10 FOR FREE

Microsoft allowed owners of Windows 7 and Windows 8 to upgrade to Windows 10 for free in the first year of Windows 10's release, but, now that grace period has passed, most people will need to pay for Windows 10. However, there is a way to still upgrade to Windows 10 for free.

Above: Users who need assistive technologies can still download Windows 10 for free.

Above: Windows 10 Anniversary Update can be downloaded right now from Microsoft's website.

Microsoft still offers a free version of Windows 10 from its accessibility website at www.microsoft.com/en-us/accessibility/windows10upgrade. Click the 'Upgrade Now' button and a tool will download that will take you through the installation process. *However*, this method is designed for people who use assistive technologies to use Windows with their disability, so while anyone can use this method, you may have to square it with your conscience if you don't need assistive technologies. Microsoft may also remove this free offer at any time.

How to Download the Windows 10 Anniversary Update

The Windows 10 Anniversary Update will be rolling out for many Windows 10 owners, so you can check to see if you have the update waiting for you by opening the Start menu and going to Settings > Update & Security > Check for Updates. You can also manually download the update by going to the Windows 10 update history website at https://support.microsoft.com/en-us/help/12387/windows-10-update-history and clicking on the blue 'Get the Anniversary Update now' button. The tool will download, then just click it and follow the instructions to update Windows 10.

CREATE A WINDOWS 10 DISK

You don't have to rely on Windows Update to do the work – you can download an ISO file of Windows 10 instead.

Get the File Online

While the preferred method of installing Windows 10 is via the upgrade route, you can download an installation file. This is useful to have in case of a huge system crash and also if Windows Update isn't playing ball. To get Windows 10, head to http://www.microsoft.com/en-gb/software-download/windows10ISO

Above: You can mount Windows 10 on a USB stick as a recovery media.

Choose the Type of Windows

You first have to choose the language and then either 32 bit or 64 bit. This depends totally on the type of PC you're going to install it on. Modern PCs are mostly 64 bit, but go to the System menu on your machine to check.

Create the Media

When the file has been downloaded, open it and it will prompt you to create an installation disc. You have two choices: a blank CD or a USB stick. Choose the option, stick it in your PC and then let Windows do its work.

Hot Tip

The best way to install Windows 10 is as an update and then refresh your system using the built-in tools explained on pages 236–37.

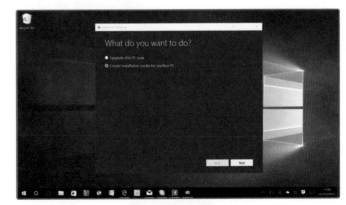

Above: When you download Windows 10 the installer does all the hard work.

GETTING STARTED

THE START MENU

Due to popular demand, Windows 10 sees the Start menu restored after it was replaced in Windows 8 – but it's been given a modern twist. Here's what you need to know.

WHAT IS THE START MENU?

The Start menu is the gatekeeper to all your programs and apps in Windows 10. It's your first port of call, and is designed to provide a quick way to your most-used content on your PC. The icon is found in the bottom left-hand corner of your PC's screen, and clicking or tapping it will fire up the menu.

Above: The Start menu has returned in Windows 10.

Why Does It Matter?

The Start menu has been a fixture of Windows since 1995 and a cornerstone of people's PC experience ever since. However, Microsoft's decision to move to the dominating Start screen in Windows 8 was met with almost universal derision, thanks to the way it disconnected the Start menu from the way people use their Windows PCs.

What Can It Do?

While the Start menu is still essentially a list of programs, apps and folders just as it was in 1995, it's now a much more powerful beast. In Windows 10 it's designed to present you with live information, change its appearance to make sure you have the options you need and, of course, save you time. It's infinitely customizable.

Start Menu Layout

The new Start menu is split into two halves. On the left-hand side is a list of static apps and programs at the top – your most-used content. At the bottom are options to open your File

Explorer, Settings menu and a list of every app and program on your PC. The right-hand side is a totally customizable list of tiles.

With the Windows 10 Anniversary Update, the Start menu has had a bit of a redesign. You'll no longer see an 'All Apps' option – instead, on the left side, you'll be presented with a full list of your applications. Scroll with your finger or mouse to view the list. At the top you'll also now see the last three apps and programs that you've installed, under 'Recently added'. You'll also see quick access buttons to File Explorer, Settings and Shut Down options on the far-left-hand side.

Check Out Live Tiles

As soon as you head to the Start menu you'll notice the right-hand side is anything but a static list of apps. The tiles are designed to present information, so your Calendar app will show your next appointment, and the Mail tile will cycle through recent subject lines of unread messages, so you can get the information you need without even opening the app.

Rename Sections

The apps on the right are split into sections and you can have as many as you like. By default the top section is called 'Life at a glance' but if you click that name, you can replace it with anything you like. You can also move the section headers anywhere you like by dragging the two lines to the right-hand side.

Delete Tiles

You might not like all the pre-determined apps that Windows places in the right-hand column, but never fear, this is Windows 10. Just right-click any unwanted tile and choose Unpin from Start to have it banished.

Add Tiles

If there's an app not in the list that really should be, then it's simple to summon it. Just go to the All Apps button at the bottom of the left column, and right-click it when you see the app in the list. Tap or click Pin to Start to have it added.

Above: You can now resize the Start menu.

Drag Tiles

You'll definitely want to reorder your ensemble of apps in the right-hand column, and that's easy to do as well. Just click and hold (or tap and hold, touch-screen people) and you can drag the apps around the Start menu. You'll notice that they snap into place; a little tinkering and you can get them all perfectly arranged to your taste.

Resize Tiles

Not all tiles are made equal, and you can choose to have some bigger than others, so as to reflect their importance – email might be made bigger than Super Pinball DX, for example. To change a tile's size, just right-click and choose between small, medium or large.

Resize the Start Menu

The Start menu's entire size can be changed to suit your tastes. You can hover your mouse over the right-hand edge and drag it out to double its size. You can also change it from the top, where you can actually fine-tune the size of the window too.

Above: Customize the Start Menu with your choice of colour.

See Your Most-Used Apps

Your most frequently used applications are listed in the Most used column in the middle left of the Start menu. You can remove these from the list by right-clicking and choosing More > Don't show in this list. However, you can't add apps or re-order them – Windows 10 will decide that for you.

Change the Start Menu Colour

The Start menu doesn't have to be in the colour that shows up when you load Windows 10 for the first time. You can pick from the range of Windows colours by right-clicking (or pressing and holding) on the desktop and choosing Personalize. Then tap or click Colours from the list. Turn off the option to automatically select colours and then choose one from the swatches.

Go Back to Windows 8 Style

The new Start menu is designed to fit in one pane, but you can go back to the old full-screen Windows 8 style, if that's what you prefer. Right-click or tap and hold on the desktop, choose

Above: You can still have the Start menu go full-screen.

Personalize and then Start. Click or tap the switch to Use Start full screen to have it change.

Stop the Start Menu Being So Responsive
If the Live Tiles are a bit too much for you to deal with, then you can calm things down by making them flat again. Just right-click a tile and then choose Turn live tile off. Just reverse the process to turn them on again.

Use the Start Menu as a Shortcut
If you right-click on the Start menu, you get access to even more shortcuts. These include individual and commonly used settings menus, such as Control Panel, System and Programs and Features – among a host of more complex and lesser-used options.

Programs and Features
Mobility Centre
Power Options
Event Viewer
System
Device Manager
Network Connections
Disk Management
Computer Management
Command Prompt
Command Prompt (Admin)

Task Manager
Control Panel
File Explorer
Search
Run

Shut down or sign out
Desktop

Above: Right-clicking on the Start Menu takes you to a host of further options.

THE DESKTOP

The Windows desktop is a big space to open all your files and documents, and is effectively the place you do all your tasks. It can hold unsorted files and folders while you work on them, as well as all your files arranged under icons.

CHANGING DESKTOP BACKGROUND PICTURE

The most noticeable thing about the desktop is the background picture – which is probably the first thing you'll want to change. To select a new one from the pre-installed list, just right-click the desktop, select Personalize and then choose from the pictures. Alternatively you can add any of your photos to the desktop by right-clicking on the file and choosing Set as desktop background.

How to Change the Theme

Themes are complementary sets of pre-ordained colours with a desktop background for those who like a designer's touch. Search 'theme settings' in the Cortana box and choose any combination. If you have your PC just how you like it, you can save your current setup for future posterity by clicking Save Theme.

The Windows 10 Anniversary Update brings a new dark theme to Windows, which lets you change the appearance of apps to match darker backgrounds. To enable this mode, open the Start menu and click on Settings > Personalisation > Colors. In the screen that appears you'll

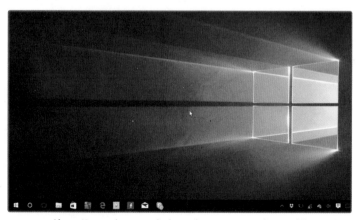

Above: You can choose your background picture to personalize your PC.

see an option that says 'Choose your app mode', allowing you to choose between Light and Dark.

Change Your Screensaver

Screensavers used to prevent old CRT monitors burning out, and now they're just nice things that appear when you walk away from your PC. Change yours by searching 'screensaver' in Cortana and then choosing the option from the list. Choose a screensaver from the drop-down menu and click preview. Yes, they're still exactly the same as Windows XP.

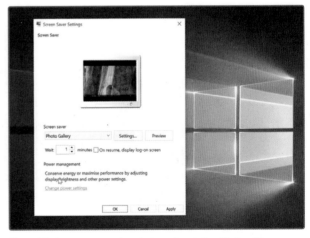

Above: There are preset themes of complimentary colours for all elements of Windows 10.

Organize Your Icons

The desktop is home to icons, and while it's arguably better to file them elsewhere (more on that later), you can keep them in check on your desktop. Right-click the desktop and choose Sort By to change the order your icons appear. If you just want to bring order to the chaos without changing your icons' arrangement, you can right-click and choose View and Align Icons to grid.

Above: Windows screensavers haven't changed much since Windows XP.

Create a New Folder

You can add multiple files to a folder straight from the desktop. Right-click anywhere and choose New > Folder. When your folder is created you have the chance to name it,

Above: Right-click on the desktop to quickly arrange icons.

Above: You can now have more than one desktop set up how you wish.

and you can then drag files into it. If you want to rename it later, just right-click and choose Rename.

VIRTUAL DESKTOP

A brand new feature in Windows 10 lets you have multiple desktops at the same time. Here's why and, more importantly, how.

What Are Virtual Desktops?

Virtual desktops are a new feature in Windows 10. It's essentially the ability to create multiple desktops, so you can group different sets of tasks together. It's been an add-on to Windows for a while, but this is the first time the feature has come built in.

Why Should You Use Them?

Some people find using virtual desktops helps them work better. For example, you could have a desktop for web browsing and social media and another for work, to keep distractions out of your eyeline.

How to Create a Second Virtual Desktop

There's a new item on the taskbar called Task View. Click or tap that menu and a new overlay will appear with your current windows spread out and the desktop below. Click or tap the New desktop icon in the bottom right and a new desktop will appear. Tap that desktop to go to it. A new, clean desktop will appear.

Switch Between Desktops

When you want to switch back, you can just tap Task View again and select the original desktop. However, if you're a fan of desktop shortcuts you can hit the Windows key + Tab to open that window. If you want to stick with the keyboard, hit Tab again – this time on its own to flick down to the desktop list. The left and the right keys will switch and Enter will select.

Move Programs Between Desktops

You can only have programs open on one desktop at a time, otherwise things would get confusing. However, you can move a program between desktops, if you wish. Just tap or click the Task View (or hit the Windows key + Tab) and then find the program in the top pane you wish to move. Right-click it, tap or click Move to and then the desktop destination.

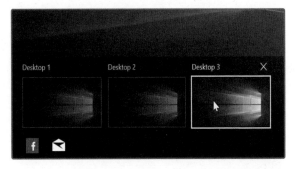

Above: You can switch between desktops using the Windows Key + Tab.

With the Anniversary Update, you can now pin certain windows so they appear in every virtual desktop. Right click on a window in the Task View and select 'Show this window on all desktops'.

How to Remove a Virtual Desktop

If you want to close a desktop, just open Task View again from the taskbar or Windows key + Tab. Select the close icon (X) over the desktop. Any programs or apps that are open on that desktop will jump over to the original one, so you won't lose any work. If you don't want to see them, make sure you close them first.

THE TASKBAR

The taskbar in Windows 10 is a huge part of the operating system, containing many component parts. The taskbar runs along the bottom of the Windows 10 desktop and puts all your apps and programs at your fingertips.

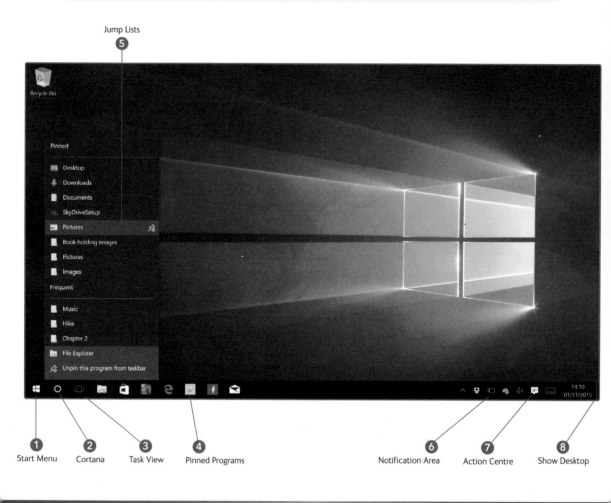

Jump Lists
5

Pinned

Desktop
Downloads
Documents
SkyDriveSetup
Pictures
Book holding images
Pictures
Images

Frequent

Music
Hike
Chapter 2
File Explorer
Unpin this program from taskbar

Recycle Bin

14.10
01/11/2015

1 Start Menu   2 Cortana   3 Task View   4 Pinned Programs   6 Notification Area   7 Action Centre   8 Show Desktop

A TOUR OF THE TASKBAR

The taskbar is a very familiar feature in Windows, but this latest version has some new touches in addition to the tried and tested.

1 Start Menu

The Start menu lives on the far left of the taskbar, which is a quick way to access your most-used apps, programs and files. Right-click the Start menu for faster access to frequently used settings menus.

2 Cortana

Cortana is a brand new addition to Windows 10, and is the virtual voice assistant for your PC. You can search to find everything from files and Windows options to web queries; you can also speak your commands. Turn to pages 51–57 for a full guide to Cortana.

3 Task View

Task View is another new addition to the Windows 10 taskbar, which controls new virtual desktops. Turn to pages 42–43 for a full guide to virtual desktops.

4 Pinned Programs

The taskbar's main job is to be a home for all your programs. Any program that's currently being run will appear as an icon on the taskbar, and you can pin them there permanently. To pin programs or apps to the taskbar, you can drag them into place or just right-click the icon and press Pin this program to taskbar.

5 Jump Lists

When a program or app is on the taskbar, you can right-click the menu to access options. What's more, you can pin files or options into place. Hover over any option in a Jump List and press the pin icon to store in the list permanently.

Hot Tip

Just click the circle, press the Windows key + S or say 'Hey Cortana'.

Notification Area

The notification area (a.k.a. system tray) in Windows 10 is home to important system information such as the clock, battery level and wireless network connectivity – as well as a whole load of nonsense you don't need. Right-click the taskbar and choose Properties. Click Customize and then select which icons appear on the taskbar. Don't be afraid to cull. The Windows 10 Anniversary Update has made the clock in the taskbar much more useful as well. Now when you click on the time and date it brings up your calendar, along with any upcoming events. You can add an event by pressing the '+' icon. The volume menu has also been boosted, and it now allows you to quickly switch between audio devices, such as speakers and headphones.

⑦ **Action Centre**

The Action Centre in Windows 10 puts important system notifications and a bunch of customizable options at your fingertips. Check out our guide on pages 49–51.

Above: Windows 10 now puts all notifications in one place.

⑧ **Show Desktop**

Easy to miss is the discreet Show Desktop button on the far right. Click this to clear everything off the desktop, and again to bring it all back just as it was.

Above: You can quickly change the master volume from the taskbar.

LOGGING IN

There are several different ways to log into Windows 10, which offer varying levels of security. You can use a PIN, a picture or just a good old-fashioned password.

LOGGING IN FOR THE FIRST TIME

The new style Windows runs on an online Microsoft account, which Windows 8 users should already have. If you're upgrading your PC from Windows 7, your PC will create a temporary account, which you will need to upgrade later. Read on to find out how.

Create a Microsoft Account

If you're firing up Windows 10 for the first time then a box will appear for you to type in an email address. This can be for an existing Microsoft account (Hotmail, Live, Xbox account etc.) or any email address, which will then become a Windows ID.

If you don't want to create a Microsoft ID at this stage, you can click Sign in without a Microsoft account at the bottom – but large amounts of Windows 10 will be off-limits.

Use a Windows Hello PIN

Windows 10 features a new feature called Windows Hello. It's essentially a PIN that can be

Above: Windows Hello lets you use a PIN instead of a password.

used as a faster way of logging into your PC and downloading apps from the Windows Store. Here's how to set up Windows Hello.

1. Search for 'sign in options' in Cortana or go to Settings > Accounts > Sign-in options.

2. Go to Change your PIN.

3. Press OK to apply.

Picture Password

In Windows 10 you can use a Picture Password instead of having to type in a password or PIN. You can use any image and then designate a number of hidden invisible spots, which you can select to log in. Just tap or click this secret combination on the image and you can access your PC. It's great for touch-screen devices without a keyboard.

Below: You can use a picture to avoid long passwords.

Logging Out and Shutting Down

To log out of Windows just click or tap the Start icon, click your account name at the top of the menu and choose Sign out.

Switch Users

If you have multiple accounts, you can switch between them from the Start menu. Click your account name and then choose a user from the list.

THE WINDOWS 10 ACTION CENTRE

Just like smartphones have places for all your notifications, now so does Windows 10. In older versions of Windows this was just a place for nagging messages to update this or that, but now it's home to alerts about new emails, Facebook posts and other notifications.

MANAGING NOTIFICATIONS

Once you start using apps, the Action Centre will start getting busier, so it's a good idea to keep on top of the messages. You can kill any message by clicking the X button, and hitting Clear All will rid your PC of the whole lot. Notifications have been given an overhaul in the Anniversary Update. You can easily dismiss notifications by clicking the middle button (or scroll wheel) of your mouse, and you can also dismiss all notifications from a certain application by middle-clicking the name of the app.

Choose What You See

1. Type 'settings' into the Search bar and select System > Notifications and actions. Using the sliders you can determine whether to Show app notifications and whether to Show notifications on the lock screen.

2. At the bottom, you'll see a list of called Show notifications from these apps. Flick the slider to the off position for any you don't wish to receive alerts from.

3. Click an individual app to fine-tune notifications.

Above: The Action Centre features a host of quick options to avoid dealing with the Settings menu.

Above: In Notifications and actions you can manage what notifications you receive in the Action Centre.

Edit the Quick Actions

At the bottom of the Action Centre menu is a series of buttons, which you can use to access Windows settings more quickly. You can control the placement of these, to put the things you need within reach. This also lets you keep your Notification Area free. Follow these steps to choose yours.

1. Type 'settings' into the Search bar and select System > Notifications and actions.

2. Tap one of the quick action icons.

3. Choose an item from the list.

4. Repeat for the other items and then tap the Action Centre to see them in place.

Above: You can edit the quick actions to put your most common options within easy reach.

CORTANA

Cortana is a part of Windows that's actually trickled down from Microsoft's mobile phones. Brand new to Windows 10, Cortana is your personal assistant, here to help you with a multitude of tasks from search to sports.

WHAT IS CORTANA?

Cortana is a voice-activated personal assistant and search tool that aims to do way more than just find files on your PC. It's designed to help you find anything from files to web searches, and aims to interpret what you need and help you find it right from the desktop.

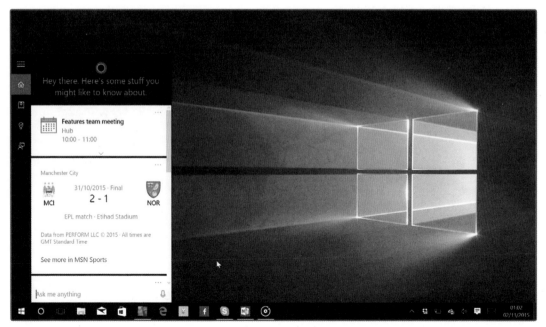

Above: Cortana is the new way to search your PC.

What Can Cortana Do?

As well as searching for things, Cortana also helps you to complete tasks on your Windows 10 PC more quickly. It can add things to your calendar, set reminders, identify a song that's playing, do quick sums, check the weather and send emails. It's pretty amazing stuff and it lives on your taskbar.

How Does Cortana Work?

You can start Cortana in a number of ways. Firstly, you can turn on the voice assistant elements (see below) and just say 'Hey Cortana' to get started. However, that's not always the best way to get what you need. You can also search more traditionally by clicking into the box and typing your search, or just press the Windows key and start typing.

How to Turn On Voice Search

1. Click the Cortana icon on the taskbar to get started.

2. Click the Settings icon.

3. Choose the Notebook icon.

4. Scroll down to Hey Cortana and turn on Let Cortana respond to 'Hey Cortana'.

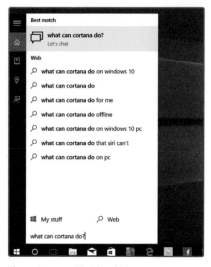

Above: Cortana will find files, folders and even search the web.

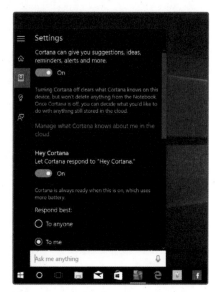

Above: You can say 'Hey Cortana' to search with your voice.

Above: You can train Cortana to know your voice better.

Above: Try searching for files instead of trawling through folders.

How to Train Cortana

As Cortana listens for your voice commands it needs to understand what you're saying. Voice recognition has come a long way and Cortana is one of the best, but you can perform a short training session to fine-tune it to your voice. To start training Cortana, go back to the Settings menu (as above) and choose Learn my Voice from the same menu.

Search for Files and Apps

If you're looking for a file, document or app, there's no need to even leave the desktop – you can ask Cortana instead. Just start typing the name of a file into the search bar and results will start to auto-complete in the main window.

You can then start making the search more advanced within Cortana. You can click or tap the My Stuff option to open all matching results. You can then filter what you see by choosing the drop-down option called Sort to switch between the most relevant or most recent options.

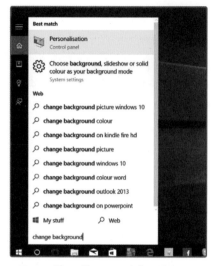

Above: You can search for settings options such as 'connect to Wi-Fi'.

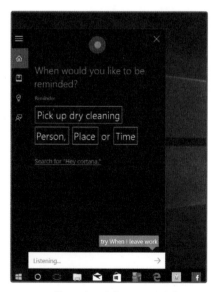

Above: Just ask Cortana to remind you of something and set a time.

With the recent Windows 10 Anniversary Update, Cortana is now more useful than ever before.

It has been fitted with a host of new features that makes using your Windows 10 device incredibly easy – and all you need to do is use your voice to get started.

Search the Web

You can also search the web from Cortana. Just type in what you're looking for, and your query will appear at the top. What's more, related searches will appear below offering alternative ideas and popular searches, which may help you find what you need. Results from the Windows Store will also appear in the list.

Set a Reminder

You can quickly set reminders in Cortana without the hassle of firing up a calendar or app. Type or say, 'Remind me to email Rachel at 6 p.m.'. You can then start fine-tuning the reminder to be on specific days, times, have it recur and even pop up when you arrive or leave a specific place.

Avoid Clashes in Your Calendar

Cortana will alert you if any reminders or appointments clash with ones already in your calendar. If they do, you'll be asked if you want to re-schedule one of the events. Cortana can also identify what sort of appointment you make, so if you're meeting someone for lunch Cortana can ask you if you want to book a table or if you need directions to the restaurant.

Check Notifications

When you start building up a body of reminders, you can see all of them in the Reminders tab. Just click on the Cortana search box and click the light-bulb icon to get a list of all current reminders. You can also delete them from this menu, but they can't be edited.

Use Cortana in Your Browser

Cortana is built into Microsoft's new Edge browser too. We go into Edge in full depth over on pages 128–37, but for now we'll just tell you that if you highlight any word or phrase you can right-click and 'Ask Cortana'. A new window will pop up in the right-hand side, which will define the word or pull in web searches to help you find out more.

Above: Allow Cortana to use your location to personalize recommendations.

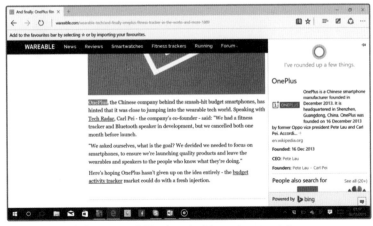

Above: Cortana is built into Microsoft Edge. Just right-click a word to get started.

Hot Tip

Try '30GBP in USD' or other currencies, weights or measures to get instant conversions.

Identify Music

Cortana does a mean impression of Shazam (a music identification app). Say the command (typing won't work) 'What is this song?' and Cortana will use your microphone to listen to the music and match it to a specific song. You can then choose to buy it through the Windows Store.

Above: Cortana can help with maths problems too; just type a sum to get the answer.

Make Cortana Work With Google Chrome

Cortana defaults to using the Windows Edge browser and Bing as a search engine, but you can trick it to use Google. In Google Chrome download the Chrometana extension. Cortana will use Chrome happily but only to use Bing. Chrometana will automatically redirect that search to Google instead.

Tell Cortana What You Like

As well as doing all the nifty search stuff, Cortana can also provide you with information on things like restaurants, films to watch and even more. However, to do that, it needs a bit of help.

Go to the Notebook by clicking in the box and choosing the second icon down, and you will see a full list of Cortana features.

Above: Tell Cortana about your interests to get better information.

Above: Cortana will give you local weather reports.

Above: Ask Cortana for a joke, and you may get a surprise.

Send Text Messages

Cortana can also be used to compose and send text messages. You'll either need a smartphone running Windows 10 mobile or an Android device with the Cortana app installed. (To install the app, open up the Google Play Store on your smartphone and search for 'Cortana'; see pages 94–95 for more details on this).

In the Cortana app, tap on Sync notifications, then turn on 'Missed call notifications,' 'Incoming message notifications' and 'App notifications sync.'

On your Windows 10 device click on Cortana's search box and select the Cog icon to open up settings and select 'Send notifications between devices'.

All you need to do is say 'Hey Cortana, text' followed by the name of the contact you want to send a message to. You can dictate the text message and then say 'Send' when you're done.

Use Cortana From Your Lock Screen

Another handy new feature included in the Windows 10 Anniversary Update is the ability to use Cortana without having to unlock your screen.

Just say 'Hey Cortana' and it'll start listening – so if you're heading to the airport, all you need to do is ask what time your flight number departs, and Cortana will respond.

SETTINGS

You could write a book about the Control Panel alone and its myriad of sections and options, but over the course of this guide most areas will be fully explored. The new Settings menu now performs the role of the traditional Control Panel, offering key Windows options accessible via Cortana and the Start menu.

ACCESS SETTINGS

Fans of the desktop can still use the classic Control Panel. The easiest way to access it is to right-click the Start menu and then choose it from the list. It contains the same options as the Settings menu, but will be more familiar to long-time Windows users.

Above: The new Settings menu offers a host of Windows tools.

Find Out More About Your System

To get a full overview of your system, click System > About > System info in the Settings menu. You can also access the same menu via the Control Panel > System, or search 'system information' in Cortana. Here you can get a digestible look at all your PC's essential information, such as:

Above: The Settings screen can be accessed from the Start menu.

- ◯ Your version of Windows 10
- ◯ The processor type and speed
- ◯ RAM
- ◯ Graphics card
- ◯ Activation status

You can also change the name of your PC here. In the System menu click or tap Change Settings in the Computer name section. You can then set a computer description, which is essential when you have more than one in your house. You can also rename your PC in this menu.

Above: System Info is the easiest way to find information about your PC.

POWER OPTIONS

A neat set of options can be found in Control Panel > System and Security > Power options. From here you can tweak settings such as deciding how long your screen stays on for before it enters standby and choosing whether you need to enter your password when it wakes up.

Above: Power plans can speed up your PC or extend your battery.

Above: Changing the screen resolution will adapt the way Windows looks on different sized displays.

Create a Custom Power Plan

To create your own custom plan, open the Power Options menu and tap or click Create a power plan. You can base your plan on an existing one, so if you want your custom setting to be heavy on power, choose High Performance. Name your setting and press next. You can then choose a combination of display, sleep and screen settings to conserve power. Select Create to finish. In the Windows 10 Anniversary Update you now also have more control over what apps can run in the background. Limiting these apps will help you preserve battery life. To access these options go to Settings > System > Battery and choose between 'Always allow in background', 'Managed by Windows' and 'Never allow in background'.

ADJUST SCREEN RESOLUTION

While we've already covered most of the options in the Personalization menu in Control Panel on pages 40–41, it's perhaps the Display menu that is the more important.

From here you can adjust screen resolution, so you can optimize the appearance of your Windows 10 PC. Normally this is a case of moving the slider up to maximum, but if you're changing monitors or plugging your PC into a TV, for example, this is a crucial settings option.

Change Text Size

You can change the size of fonts in Windows 10 in the Personalization menu. There's a drop-down box for the type of font you want to change – for example menus, icons or message boxes – and a second menu to the right for the text size. Press Apply when you're happy to make the change.

CHANGE THE TIME AND DATE

Unlike the old days, Windows 10 will change the clock automatically when you connect to the Internet, but sometimes you will need to reset the clock. Having the incorrect time can prevent crucial Windows features from working properly.

You can change the time in the Clock, Language and Region settings in the Control Panel. Click the option and choose Set time and date. Click that option and then Change date and time. You can then make adjustments before clicking Apply.

Change Time Zone

Back in the Set date and time

Above: You can change the time and time zone of your PC when you go on holiday.

menu you can change the time zone – handy if you're a jet-setter. Just click Change time zone and choose the correct option.

Alternatively you can add a second time zone, which is great for those working with people overseas. Click the Additional Clocks tab at the top of the menu and then check the Show this clock box. Set your second time zone and click Apply.

MAKE WINDOWS EASIER TO USE

If you find using Windows awkward owing to poor eyesight or due to difficulties using your mouse or touch screen, there are heaps of tools in Windows 10 to make the experience easier.

THE EASE OF ACCESS CENTRE

To find these features just head to Settings > Ease of Access and make the following adjustments.

Above: The Ease of Access Centre makes Windows easier for people to use.

Make Your Screen Easier to See

1. Find the Ease of Access Centre in Control Panel and then Make the computer easier to see.

2. Check the magnifier. This is a tool that enlarges parts of your screen so that you can see words and images more clearly.

3. Click Choose a high contrast theme, which can make text easier to read.

Make Using the Mouse Easier

For some people, using a mouse isn't easy. So, while the new user is getting used to this alien tool, the mouse can be made easier to use in the Ease of Access Centre.

1. Change the size and colour of the pointer.

2. Turn on mouse keys to move the pointer with the direction buttons on the keyboard.

3. Click mouse settings to change the pointer speed.

Make Using the Keyboard Easier

1. If you want to customize the keyboard go back to the Ease of Access Centre and choose Change how your keyboard works.

Above: If you find using the mouse difficult you can change the settings.

2. If you struggle with complex keyboard shortcuts such as Ctrl + Alt + Delete you can turn on Sticky Keys. This means you can press key combinations concurrently, rather than simultaneously to launch commands.

3. Toggle Keys can be activated to alert you when you press the Caps Lock, Num Lock or Scroll Lock keys. These notifications prevent what can be annoying mistakes if these keys are pressed inadvertently.

4. When you turn on Filter Keys, Windows ignores when you press the same key rapidly or when you press keys for several seconds unintentionally.

Above: The on-screen keyboard enables you to type without hardware.

SECURITY

For all its life-changing benefits, the Internet is also a place full of malware, scammers and snoopers, which can at best slow down your PC's performance, and at worst devastate your files and steal your private information. Here's how to secure your Windows 10 PC.

LOCK DOWN YOUR PC

The key way of locking down your PC is to stop people physically accessing it if it's lost or stolen. Luckily in Windows 10, there are more ways than ever.

Set a Password

Your Windows ID offers a simple way to lock down your PC. When you turn on, your computer will prompt you for a password. If you don't currently have password-protection turned on, follow these steps.

1. From Cortana search for 'sign in options' and hit enter.

2. Under password, choose Change.

3. Type in your password; you'll be asked to enter it twice.

You can also change when you're prompted for your password. By default, if your PC goes to sleep you don't need to enter it to wake it up.

Above: You can force Windows to make someone enter a password to wake your PC from sleep.

You can boost security by adding a password on wake-up. In the Sign-in options screen you can change the Require sign-in drop-down box from 'Never' to 'When PC wakes up from sleep'.

Add a PIN

A new feature in Windows 10 is the PIN. This is beneficial for a number of reasons. Entering four digits is less hassle than a long password, and it means your PC won't have the same code as the gateway to your email, online storage and more.

1. To set a PIN go back to the Sign-in options menu.

2. Click Set PIN and choose four numbers.

3. Repeat the PIN and click Next.

Above: PINs are faster and safer than passwords.

Use Windows Hello

If your PC has a fingerprint reader, which many do now, you can use Windows Hello to sign into your PC. This is a new super-secure feature of Windows 10. To set it up, go to Sign-in options and under Windows Hello, you'll see options for face, fingerprint or iris. This will only appear if you have the requisite hardware.

Since the Windows 10 Anniversary Update, Windows Hello has been made even more useful, as you can now use it to securely log into apps and websites using the Edge browser. With a quick scan of your fingerprint or eye (with a compatible webcam such as an Intel RealSense camera) you'll have secure access to your favourite apps.

Above: Fingerprint readers are the height of security for modern-day PC users.

KEEP SAFE FROM MALWARE

Keeping viruses, spyware and trojans (collectively known as malware) out of your PC is essential. While buying specialist protection used to be the norm for PC users, there is now adequate protection built into Windows 10. Here's how to use it.

Check Your Security Options

If you have bought a new PC, then you might have an antivirus trial already on it. This can cause all kind of problems, so if you don't intend to use it, you must get rid of it.

To check what's installed, type 'security' into Cortana and choose Check security status. Click down on the Security tab and check what is listed for virus protection, network firewall and spyware. If it's a pre-installed trial, then you will need to remove it. Turn to page 240 to find out how.

Security and Maintenance	— □ ×
↑ ✔ › Control Panel › System and Security › Security and Maintenance	⌄ ↻ Search Control Panel 🔍

Control Panel Home

Change Security and Maintenance settings

Change User Account Control settings

Change Windows SmartScreen settings

View archived messages

Review recent messages and resolve problems

Security and Maintenance has detected one or more issues for you to review.

Security   ⌃

Network firewall   On
    Windows Firewall is actively protecting your PC.

Virus protection   On
    AVG AntiVirus Free Edition is turned on.

Spyware and unwanted software protection   On
    AVG AntiVirus Free Edition is turned on.

Internet security settings   OK
    All Internet security settings are set to their recommended levels.

User Account Control   On
    UAC will notify you when applications try to make changes to the computer.
    Change settings

Windows SmartScreen   On
    Windows SmartScreen is helping to protect your PC from unrecognised applications and files downloaded from the Internet.
    Change settings

See also
File History
Windows Program Compatibility Troubleshooter

Above: The Security and Maintenance window lets you check your PC's coverage.

WINDOWS DEFENDER

First it's important to check that Windows Defender is turned on and working properly. As ever, from Cortana just type 'defender' and then choose the program from the results.

Windows Defender uses a traffic-light system to tell you what's going on: if the top bar is green and there's a tick on the computer screen graphic then everything is good; if there's another colour, there's work to do.

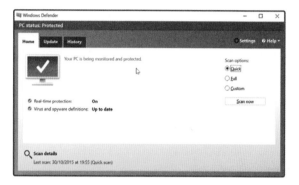

Above: Windows Defender is the built-in anti-malware tool.

Check the Status

There are two status lines in the main screen. The first says Real-time protection which should say 'on' and the second is Virus and spyware definitions, which should say 'up to date'. If either of those two statuses is incorrect, you'll need to take action.

Update Windows Defender

This should be done automatically in Windows 10 to make sure you have the latest protection, but problems can occur. To update manually go to Windows Defender and click the Update tab.

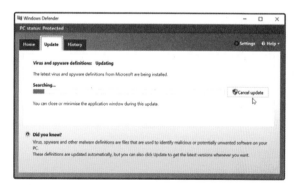

Above: Make sure you keep Defender updated against the latest threats.

Run a Scan

Windows Defender also has the ability to scan your PC for malware. To run a scan of your PC, look to the right of the Windows Defender where you'll see a box with scanning options. A quick scan only looks in critical folders on your PC. The second is a full scan, which will take its time searching every file on your computer, looking for any suspect files.

Limited Periodic Scanning

Usually, running more than one anti-virus program is not recommended, as they could conflict with each other. However, with Windows 10 Anniversary a new feature called Limited Periodic Scanning lets you take advantage of Windows Defender

Above: You can now benefit from Windows Defender even if you use another anti-virus program.

alongside other anti-virus programs. To turn it on, type 'Settings' into the Start Menu, go to Update & security > Windows Defender and click the toggle under 'Limited Periodic Scanning'.

Set Up Windows Firewall

As well as Defender, Windows has its own Firewall too. Not something that has to be tinkered with too much, it simply needs to be turned on. You can check by searching 'firewall' in Cortana, and choosing Windows Firewall. You can turn Windows Firewall on or off in the left-hand column – but you should leave it on unless you're using another product.

SECURE YOUR PRIVACY

The nature of cloud computing means the sharing of a lot of data, but if you want to keep your private information out of the hands of big companies, including Microsoft, here are some ways to make Windows 10 more private, although you will lose out on certain features.

Disconnect Your Account

To keep your data truly private, you can't use a Windows ID to sign into your PC. In Cortana search for 'your account' and choose Sign in with a local account instead. This will disconnect your Windows ID, but will limit access to cloud options such as storage and email.

Above: You don't have to use a Microsoft ID to sign into your PC.

Turning Off Diagnostics

Search for 'privacy settings' in Cortana. In the Feedback and Diagnostics tab turn Feedback & Diagnostics and Feedback Frequency to 'never' and Diagnostic and Usage Data to 'basic'.

Turn Off Advertising ID

In the Privacy settings menu you can also turn off advertising tracking and stop websites from accessing your language settings. For even more privacy, turn off all the options in the General tab.

Give Edge a Privacy Boost

In the Edge browser click the three dots and choose Settings and then Advanced Settings. Scroll down for privacy options, where there are some key improvements you can make. Firstly, you can turn on Do not track and block cookies, which will prevent advertisers from targeting you with adverts for things you might have searched. You can also instruct Edge not to save your passwords, which is good common sense if you share your PC with other people.

Remove Ads from the Start Menu

Many of us were happy to see the Start menu return after its absence from Windows 8, but there was a not-so-welcome change: Microsoft has now included adverts for apps in the Start menu. Thankfully, they are easy to get rid of. Open up Settings and go to Personalization > Start and click on the toggle next to 'Occasionally show suggestions in Start' to turn them off. You can also remove ads individually by right-clicking on the tile in the Start menu and selecting 'Uninstall' or 'Unpin'.

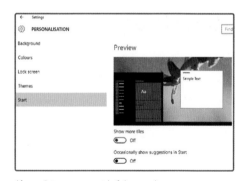

Above: It is easy to get rid of those pesky adverts on the Start menu.

Go Private

A good way to boost privacy as you browse the web is to use InPrivate browsing. While that doesn't make you invisible online, it means your browsing history, passwords and cookies won't be saved – which will at least keep the prying eyes of marketers at bay.

WINDOW SNAPPING

Windows 7 ushered in the ability to 'snap' windows side by side to make working across different apps easier. Now Windows 10 takes things to the next level.

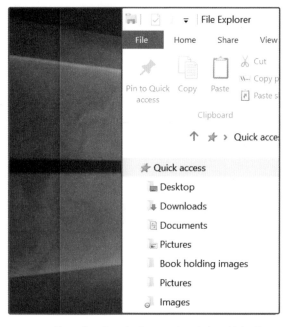

Above: Snapping makes it easy to view windows side by side.

START SNAPPING

To snap any desktop app or window just left-click its title bar (the space right at the top) and then drag it to either the left or right edge of your screen. A transparent overlay will appear, which shows you where the window is to be placed. Release the window to have it 'snap' into place.

Hot Tip

You can snap windows by using this keyboard shortcut. When a window is open press the Windows key + Left/ Right button on your keyboard. To have them snap to the corners, use the Windows key + Left + Up or Right + Down etc.

Snap Assist

When you drag a window to snap to the left or right, Windows 10 will offer up all available windows to place in the empty space. This is a new feature called Snap Assist. Just click one of the preview thumbnails to have that window placed side by side.

2×2 Snap

Window snapping has now been extended to enable you to tile up to four windows at the same time in a 2×2 grid. Take a window and with the mouse, drag and drop it into one of the four corners of the screen, and the transparent window will fall into the bottom corner. Drag and drop several windows in this way to get your 2×2 grid of open windows.

Above: Snap one window and Snap Assist will make it easy to place the next window alongside.

Fast Window Switching

When you have a lot of programs open at the same time, it can be slightly troublesome dealing with them all. You can bring any window to the fore just by clicking on its icon on the taskbar, and if a program has multiple windows, then it will show thumbnails of them all for you to select.

Above: Just press Alt+Tab to switch between windows and Virtual Desktops.

USER ACCOUNT CONTROL

A common way for malicious programs to attack your PC is to install settings without you knowing – this could be a hidden payload from something seemingly innocuous you downloaded. User Account Control (UAC) is your guardian angel.

WHAT IS UAC?

UAC is a feature in Windows 10 that forces you to manually accept any request from a program to make changes to your PC. A box will appear on the screen detailing which program is requesting to make the change, and you can allow or reject that change.

Should You Turn It Off?

When it was first introduced users were very critical of UAC, as people felt that it was continually bugging them. When you first get your Windows 10 PC, you will see more of UAC as you download programs and change settings. In daily use, however, you'll hardly see it at all.

It is possible to turn off UAC, but not advisable. It's an extremely effective tool against spyware and viruses. However, if you're finding it problematic, you can water down its efficiency, so it will only guard against the most serious changes.

User Account Control

Do you want to allow the following program to make changes to this computer?

Program name: XILab-1.8.15-win64.exe
Verified publisher: **Center of Engineering Physics, MSU Lomonosov LLC**
File origin: Hard drive on this computer

Show details

Yes   No

Change when these notifications appear

Above: User Account Control prompts when a program is attempting to make changes to your PC.

Modify UAC

Open User Account Control Settings by searching 'uac' in Cortana or accessing the settings via Control Panel > Security and Maintenance > Change User Account Control settings. Then choose between the following settings.

Above: You can turn down the severity of UAC so you will be bothered less often.

1. **Always notify**: You'll be told of a request to change Windows 10 settings. This is the setting that will require the most attention from you.

2. **Notify me when apps try to make changes**: This is the default setting and won't bother you when trusted apps want to make changes.

3. **Do not dim desktop**: The same level of notifications as level two but your PC won't be visibly affected.

4. **Never notify**: No UAC interruptions and all changes to your PC will be allowed from any application.

GETTING MICROSOFT OFFICE

One of the most common questions asked of Windows experts is regarding Office. This guide will tell you everything you need to know about getting hold of Word, Excel and the rest.

DO YOU GET OFFICE FREE IN WINDOWS 10?

A common misconception is that the desktop version of Office is a part of Windows. It's not. It's a completely separate product that Microsoft charges for, and it's a huge part of their business. As such, there's no built-in word processing or spreadsheet program in Windows 10.

Get the Universal Apps for Free

You can download free versions of Word, Excel and PowerPoint for free from the Microsoft Store. These aren't as powerful as the versions you might be used to, but certainly offer a decent set of features. To download follow these simple steps:

1. Go to the Windows Store.

2. Search for 'office'.

3. Download the Word Mobile, Excel Mobile etc. apps.

Desktop App and Office 365

If you're used to the full desktop version of Office, the mobile apps might not cut it. These desktop

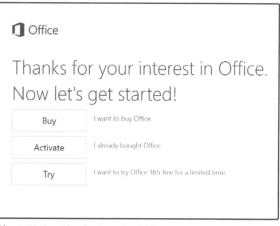

Above: Windows 10 makes it easy to get Office.

versions now come under a subscription called Office 365, which enables you to get full access for £7.99/$9.99 per month. It's a much smaller initial outlay, but you will probably pay more over the life of your PC. However, it will always be up to date.

Buy a Box Copy

You can get Office Home and Student 2016 as a single download for £120/$150 from the Microsoft Store, which means you skip the need for a subscription. You get the following desktop apps:

- Word
- Excel
- PowerPoint
- OneNote

Above: Word Mobile is a stripped-back version available for free.

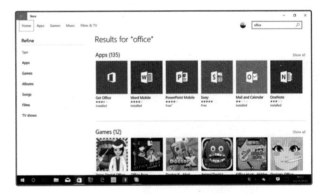

Above: Office Mobile apps are available at the Windows Store.

FREE OFFICE ALTERNATIVES

Don't want to use the free versions of Word, but don't fancy the subscriptions either? Don't fret, because there are free alternatives. They tend not to work as well, but are certainly good for the price!

- **OpenOffice:** Looks a bit like Word 2000 but is quick, clean and free.

- **Google Docs:** Not much more powerful than the free versions of Word, but it plays nicely with Word formats and the cloud storage is very neat.

MOBILE DEVICES

WINDOWS 10 ON MOBILE DEVICES

For the first time, Windows 10 brings a universal experience to all types of devices, which means you can have one operating system across your PC, tablet and phone.

INTRO TO MOBILE DEVICES

Windows 8 started to embrace tablets, but things were always a bit hit and miss. Windows 10 Mobile fixes that, but what's it all about? Read on to find out.

Below: Windows has well and truly arrived on smartphones too.

What Is Windows 10 Mobile?

Windows 10 Mobile is the company's latest operating system for mobile devices, which essentially means tablets and phones. It replaces Windows Phone and Windows 8 RT, both of which were technically different to the desktop version of Windows. That meant that, while they looked visually similar, there was still a divide between your different devices.

How Has It Changed?

The key difference between Windows 10 Mobile and Windows Phone is that there's no divide between your handset and PC. The same apps, the same notifications and everything you see on your phone will be available when you turn on your laptop.

Is It Exactly The Same?

Not quite and that's the challenge. The hardware that phones and laptops use are different, and that's been one of the problems that plagued Windows 10 tablets. What's more, you can't just shove the same OS on a phone with a 6-inch screen as a PC with a 27-inch screen.

What Can It Do?

Windows 10 Mobile does all the things you'd expect from a phone OS but it also runs apps – and that's the crucial part. Windows 10 apps are now designed to run across desktop and mobile, so you get the same experience. Before, you were essentially running two completely different versions of the same app – if it was even available on desktop and mobile, that is.

| sider Program | **Before you install** | How-to |

Supported phones for Windows 10 Mobile Insider Preview

We're working to get more Windows Phone models supported worldwide. Download the Windows Insider app, and when your phone is supported you'll be able to sign in with the same Microsoft account you used to join the Windows Insider Program. Windows 10 Mobile Insider Preview currently works with the following phones—as long as they have at least 8 GB of storage, Windows Phone 8.1 was already installed on the phone at the time of purchase, and the version number is 8.10.14219.341 or earlier.

- HTC One (M8) for Windows
- Lumia 430
- Lumia 435
- Lumia 520
- Lumia 521
- Lumia 525
- Lumia 526
- Lumia 530
- Lumia 532
- Lumia 535
- Lumia 540
- Lumia 620
- Lumia 625
- Lumia 630
- Lumia 635
- Lumia 636
- Lumia 638
- Lumia 640
- Lumia 640 XL
- Lumia 720
- Lumia 730
- Lumia 735
- Lumia 810
- Lumia 820
- Lumia 822
- Lumia 830
- Lumia 920
- Lumia 925
- Lumia 928
- Lumia 930
- Lumia 1020
- Lumia 1320
- Lumia 1520
- Lumia Icon

Notes

- Some phones, regions, and mobile operators might not support Insider Preview. If your phone isn't listed, and no preview builds appear under **Enroll** in the Windows Insider app, then your phone isn't supported and it may or may not be supported in the future.
- To see which Windows Phone operating system (OS) version is installed on your phone, go to **Settings** > **About** > **More info.**

Above: Lumia handsets will all get an upgrade to Windows 10.

How Do You Get It?

Windows 10 Mobile is a free upgrade for anyone with an older Windows Phone. That means basically any Lumia phone from the last four years, but there's a full list of compliant handsets at http://windows.microsoft.com/en-us/windows/preview-supported-phones

FLAGSHIP WINDOWS MOBILE DEVICES

Windows 10 has revealed an exciting new haul of devices designed by Microsoft. Here is the latest array of phones and tablets.

Lumia 950

The new flagship phone from Microsoft, the Lumia 950 comes with Windows 10 Mobile. It features a 5.2-inch display with a 2560 x 1440 resolution, which in terms of tech puts it right up there with any phone on the market.

Above: The new Lumia 950 is the flagship Windows 10 phone.

Above: The Lumia 950 XL offers a supersized screen.

Lumia 950 XL

The idea behind the Lumia 950 XL is a phone that can actually connect to larger displays and almost act as a laptop. It's powered by an octo-core processor (most laptops have four cores) and there's 3GB of RAM with a 1440 x 2560 QHD 5.7-inch OLED screen.

Lumia 550

Cheaper and less powerful than the two flagship Windows 10 Mobile superphones, the Lumia 550 brings the same experience for a much lower cost. You still get a 4.7-inch display, 1.1GHz quad-core processor and 1GB of RAM and it costs only £79/$99. Impressive stuff.

Surface Pro 4

Microsoft's flagship tablet has a beefy Intel Core processor yet packed into a compact 10-inch tablet, which means it can handle any computing task. It comes with its own portable keyboard, but with Bluetooth connectivity and the ability to hook up to an external monitor, it can function just as well as a desktop PC as it can a portable tablet.

Surface 3

The Surface 3 doesn't have the same power as the more expensive Surface Pro, instead opting for a low-power Intel Atom processor. It's aimed at those who just want basic browsing and apps on the move, but is smaller, lighter and you still get a portable keyboard.

Surface Book

A brand new device for Windows 10, the 13.5-inch Surface Book takes aim at portable laptops and tablets. It features a proper laptop keyboard, from which you can unclip the screen to use like a giant tablet. It's also one of the most powerful laptops you can buy, if you go for the top spec. A successor is expected in 2017.

Above: Windows 10 phones, such as the Lumia 550, can be had for as little as £79/$99.

WINDOWS 10 ON TABLETS

If you thought that using Windows 10 was about a big PC sat on your desk, then prepare to stand corrected. Windows 10 plays more nicely on tablets than ever before, and with a new set of features and modes it's easy to get started.

Above: Windows tablets radiate modernity with their sleek, minimal style.

INTRODUCTION TO TABLETS

A tablet is a touch-screen mobile device that has the processor, hard drive and internals all built into the screen. Tablets have been around for a couple of decades but were made popular by Apple's iPad, which launched in 2010.

What Kinds of Tablets Are There?

As the popularity of tablets exploded it meant that they started to diversify, and now there are devices in all shapes and sizes. By and large Windows 10 tablets are hybrids, which mean they double as laptops and tablets with detachable keyboards. There are hundreds of these on the market, from 10-inch tablets all the way up to 20-inch touch-screen desktop PCs.

Above: Windows tablets come in all shapes and sizes.

Can I Still Use a Keyboard and Mouse?

Unlike some non-Windows tablets you can use a mouse and keyboard, and many come with these peripherals built in. Windows 10 plays nicely with Bluetooth wireless devices so you can just hook these up. Obviously you can use the touch screen instead of a mouse if you wish.

Does Windows 10 Run on All Tablets?

If you have an older Windows tablet then it will upgrade just like PCs running Windows 7 or Windows 8. There are, however, some exceptions. When Windows 8 was released there were some tablets that used mobile phone technologies and ran Windows 8 RT. These devices cannot upgrade to Windows 10, although back in July 2015 Microsoft did update the OS to offer some of the latest features.

USING WINDOWS 10 TABLET MODE

Windows 10 has its own mode for tablet devices, which makes them easier to use. Here's how to get started.

What Is Tablet Mode?

When you're using Windows 10 on a touch-screen device, some elements of the operating system can be harder to use. In Windows 8 Microsoft forced everyone to use the Start screen, which was a disaster for mouse and keyboard users. This time there are no such draconian controls, but those wanting to use a tablet may want to fiddle with some settings in tablet mode.

Above: In tablet mode the Start screen goes full width.

Open Tablet Options

Many devices will go automatically into tablet mode when you detach your two-in-one PC from its dock. However, you can access the settings by searching with Cortana or going to Start > System > Tablet mode.

Above: Any Windows device can be forced into tablet mode to make it more touch friendly.

Turn On Tablet Mode

When you've arrived at this settings menu there's a button to toggle tablet mode on. Just switch the Make Windows more touch friendly button to the on position and the window will expand to fill the screen.

Touch Friendly Windows

As long as Windows 10 is in tablet mode you will only be able to access Windows apps and menus full screen, and the desktop will be off limits.

Tablet Mode Desktop Explained

1 Start menu

Instead of popping up like in the desktop version, this is now full screen like you'd find in Windows 8. There's also no button to get you back to the desktop.

2 Most used

Hit the three lines at the top to bring up the most-used apps element from the Windows 10 Start screen.

3 Back button

Cycle back to the last screen with this button on the toolbar.

Most used   Start menu   Apps list

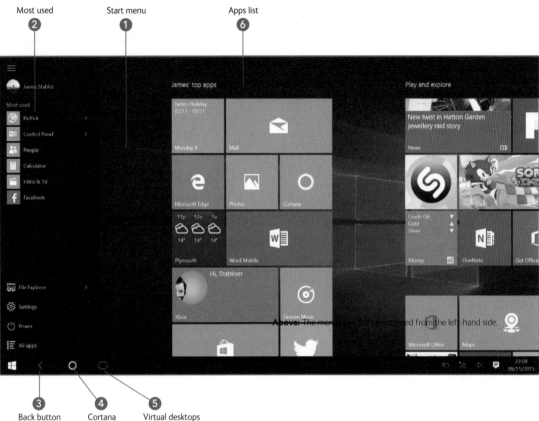

Above: The menu can still be accessed from the left-hand side.

Back button   Cortana   Virtual desktops

④ Cortana

The best way to find files, apps and settings without the traditional desktop.

⑤ Virtual desktops

You can still set up multiple desktop environments in tablet mode by hitting this button.

⑥ Apps list

Tap the list button to have quick access to the complete range of apps on your Windows 10 PC.

TABLET GESTURES

When you use your Windows 10 PC on a touch-screen device it's all about gestures with your hand. Here are the ones you need to know about.

Select or Perform an Action

Just single tap any item on screen to launch.

Get More Options

Long-press anything on screen to get more options. This essentially becomes the right-click of touch-screen windows.

Scroll Through Windows

Just place your finger on the screen and move it up, down, left or right to move the page.

Find Recently Used Apps

To see apps that are currently running, just swipe in from the left-hand edge of the screen.

Zoom In and Out

Pinch your fingers together on the screen to zoom in and separate them to zoom out.

Access the Action Centre

Swipe your finger in from the right-hand edge to reveal the Action Centre.

Close an Application

To close an app just press and hold on the title bar at the top and then drag down to the taskbar until it disappears.

WINDOWS 10 ON PHONES

Windows 10 comes to phones for the first time. Older Windows Phones get the Windows treatment, as do a raft of new flagship devices. Here's what you need to know.

INTRODUCING WINDOWS 10 PHONES

On handsets Windows 10 isn't just a smaller version of your laptop – that would be mad. Visually, it's just a minor upgrade from Windows Phone, apart from the fact that all the apps and services now work with your PC ones. This is underpinned by Microsoft OneDrive, the cloud storage service that comes as part of Windows 10.

Above: The Live Tiles on Windows 10 phones are now translucent so they do not completely block out your custom background.

Turn Your Phone Into A PC

Continuum is the new feature of Windows 10 that tailors your PC automatically to a mouse and keyboard or touch-screen input depending on what you have plugged in. It's already the part of Windows 10 that eases the transition between a laptop and tablet when you remove the keyboard, but it also works for phones.

Connect Up a Mouse and Keyboard

As you might imagine, not all older Windows phones will have the power to hook up a mouse and keyboard. However, newer devices such as the flagship Lumia 950 and 950 XL will have plenty of power to hook your smartphone up to a monitor and start using desktop apps.

Above: The Display Dock is a hardware adapter that lets you use your phone like a desktop Windows PC with keyboard, mice, and a large display.

How Do You Get It?

Windows 10 Mobile is available as an upgrade to most Lumia handsets. This will be delivered through the Windows Store. You will need to install the previous Lumia software update (Lumia Denim) before your Windows 10 Mobile one will show up.

WINDOWS 10 MOBILE FEATURES

What are the new features in Windows 10 Mobile? We run you through everything you need to know.

Design

The Windows 10 Mobile interface isn't too far off that of Windows Phone 8.1, although it has been updated to look a bit more modern. Live Tiles are translucent, so they don't completely block out custom backgrounds, and a new list of recently installed apps is now instantly accessible by swiping to the right on the home screen.

Universal Apps

Windows 10 runs apps that work across multiple types of devices. That means PCs, tablets, smartphones, even Xbox One consoles. If it runs Windows 10, the apps will work on it. They can then synchronize data between Windows 10 devices including notifications, data and even saved games (see pages 92–93 for more on this).

New Action Centre

Similar to its excellent Windows 10 counterpart, the Windows 10 Mobile Action Centre is a highly versatile menu that, in addition to listing notifications, provides quick access to and/or toggle buttons for the Camera app, Airplane Mode, WiFi settings, brightness settings, Bluetooth, torch, VPN setup tool, rotation lock and more.

Above: Windows apps can be used seamlessly across multiple devices, such as the Nokia Lumia 950 XL.

Continuum

This is the new feature in Windows 10 that enables your devices to change the way they work depending on the peripherals you attach. Continuum lets you plug your phone into an external display and use full apps with a keyboard and mouse.

Edge Browser

Windows 10 Mobile comes with its own version of the Edge browser, which is optimized for use on smaller handsets.

Notifications Across Devices

Notifications have long been a staple of mobile devices, but the Action Centre in Windows 10 Mobile means you'll get them from whichever device you're on. Get a text? You'll be notified across all devices.

Above: As part of Office on your mobile, you will have access to the invaluable Word.

Translator App

A new stock app for Windows 10 Mobile, the translator app does exactly what it says on the tin. You can perform spoken and written translation as well as the ability to point your phone's camera at signs and menus to have them deciphered for you.

Microsoft Office

A huge part of the Windows 10 Mobile experience is the legendary Microsoft Office, so you can view and amend documents on the go.

One-Handed Mode

Designed for bigger handsets like the Lumia 950 XL, the one-handed mode is enabled by pressing and holding the Start button. This will make the screen slide down so you can reach items at the top.

Reply to Messages With Your PC

When you miss a call, you can reply with a text to the person who called you right from your PC and Cortana will have your phone send it. You can just tell Cortana using voice control whom to message and the content, and she will do the rest.

Above: Being able to use Skype on your phone is a real bonus.

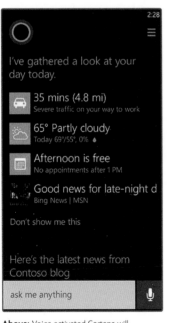

Above: Voice activated Cortana will help you when you're out and about.

Advanced Skype

Skype is now integrated into the Messaging, Phone and Skype video Windows apps, so you can use the web to communicate with your friends and family, which should save on your calls and messages.

Cortana

Cortana will remind you about things like cinema bookings and events in your calendar and even help you get there by offering directions. It even syncs with Uber so you can book a taxi straight from your home screen (see pages 94–95 for more on this).

Offline Maps

You can now save offline maps to your phone's SD card, so you don't need data access when you're navigating around foreign cities and incurring roaming charges.

UNIVERSAL APPS

The big change to Windows 10 is the all-new universal apps: whatever you do in one app will happen across all your other devices.

THIRD-PARTY APPS

Universal apps just aren't about Windows 10 tablet and laptops, but also phones and the Xbox One as well. Here's a selection of third-party apps to get you started.

Adobe Photoshop Express

While it's nothing like as powerful as the full version of Photoshop, the Express version of this popular software is still great for everyday photo touch-ups. You can quickly and easily crop, tweak and improve shots in the app. It's designed for touch screens, making it one of the more powerful mobile apps on the market.

Autodesk Pixlr

Pixlr is a picture editor full of trendy effects such as Color Splash, which accentuates objects in the image while leaving the rest black and white, there are 25 included effects, and you can download more if you sign up. Now it's available as a universal app, you can add filters and effects to your photos from any of your devices and edit them up wherever you are.

Dropbox

Like OneDrive, Dropbox is a cloud storage service that enables you to keep files online. The universal Windows app enables you to upload and view documents and photos from any of your Windows devices, as well as favouriting items. You can also set folders to auto-sync with the service. Dropbox is slightly less essential as a service now OneDrive is on the scene, but for existing users it's a hugely useful app.

Flipboard

The coolest way to read the news on your Windows 10 devices, Flipboard's app lets you create personalized magazine subscriptions and access ones made on other devices. Browse articles with a swipe of a finger and save articles for reading later on which ever device you use.

Fitbit

This fitness tracker can be used across any Windows 10 device. Get details of your steps and sleep quality while logging food and exercise verbally using Cortana. The universal app also means that nudges and achievements are delivered in your device's Action Centre.

Netflix

Possibly the perfect universal app, you will see your Netflix history and recommendations as soon as you fire up any of your Windows 10 devices. You can just put one device down (including the Xbox One) and pick up another for the same experience.

Sonic Dash

Sonic is available for all Windows devices, so you can pick up and play this famous games franchise on your PC, phone or TV and jump straight back into the action at any time.

TV Catchup

The best way to watch live TV on your PC, TV Catchup is like a Freeview box in a universal desktop app. Flick between the UK's national TV channels BBC1, BBC2, ITV1, Channel 4 and Channel 5, in addition to movies, sports, news and music channels.

Words With Friends

One of the most popular mobile games on the Windows platform, Words With Friends is now available on even more devices. Face off against far-flung pals and chat in game while you play – and of course, there's no need to be glued to your PC waiting for their turn: you'll be notified using the Windows 10 Action Centre and you're free to pick up the action on any device.

CORTANA FOR ANDROID

You no longer need to have a Windows Phone to make use of Cortana, as you can now get the Cortana app for Android devices.

GET CORTANA

To make use of Cortana on your Android smartphone, open up the Google Play Store on your device and search for 'Cortana'. Tap on 'Install' to download it to your phone.

You'll need to sign in to the same Microsoft account you use to log in to Windows 10, and once you're done, you can view texts and other notifications from your smartphone on your Windows 10 desktop. You can even reply to texts directly from Windows 10 without having to reach for your phone!

Find Your Lost Phone

A new feature of Cortana will help you find your phone if you lose it. It can detect the GPS signal of the phone and use that information to show its location on a map. You can also remotely tell your phone to ring if it's somewhere nearby, allowing you to quickly find your misplaced handset.

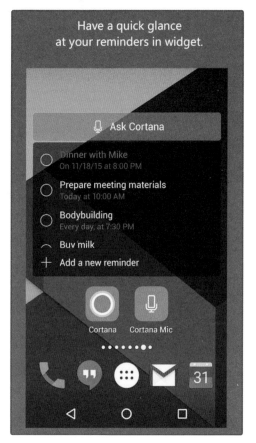

Below: Good news for Android owners! Cortana is now available on your tablets and smartphones.

Get Directions

You can ask Cortana in Windows 10 to give you directions to an address or point of interest and a map will display showing you where to go and how long it will take due to traffic. This is all very useful, but you can't very well lug your PC or laptop into your car and start driving. The good news is that with your smartphone connected to the Cortana app, the same directions will appear on your handheld device as well.

Below: Cortana can show you directions on your Windows 10 PC, as well as send them to your smartphone.

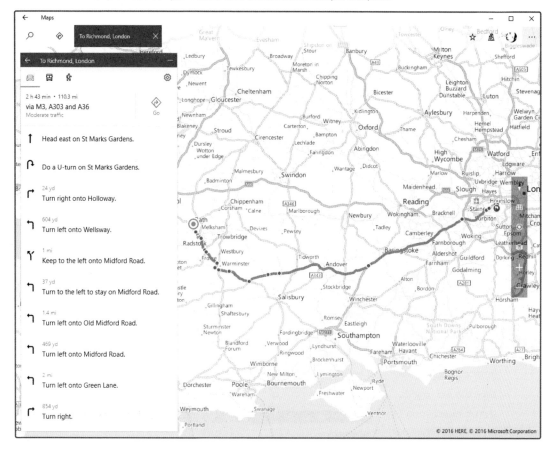

WINDOWS 10 PHONE COMPANION

Windows 10 has an app to help you get your PC working with your phone, whichever operating system you use. Android and iPhone users – this is for you.

START OFF WITH PHONE COMPANION

Phone Companion helps get your iPhone or Android phone working with Windows 10. Here's how to get started.

Above: Windows 10 plays nicely with any brand of handset.

What Does It Do?

While Windows 10 users who upgrade their handset to Windows 10 Mobile will get a seamless experience, that doesn't help people with other handsets. A lot of the apps used in Windows 10 are actually available in other app stores. While Windows 10's Phone Companion app doesn't quite do all the work for you yet, it's worth firing up to get the apps you need.

How to Start Phone Companion

To get started, just search for 'phone companion' using Cortana or search for it in the apps list in the Start menu. The next step is to plug your phone into your Windows 10 PC with the USB cable. You will see it recognized at the bottom, and you can click the bar to get status information on your handset.

Above: Plug your phone in via USB for immediate options

Supported Handsets

Windows 10's Phone Companion app works with iOS and Android phones. There is an option for Windows Phones in the list, which will just give you the good news that you already have all the apps required for a seamless Windows experience.

What Can Phone Companion Do?

1. **Get Cortana on your device**: Enables you to use Cortana on your mobile device outside of Windows 10.

2. **Automatically sync camera photos with OneDrive**: You can set your iPhone/Android handset to automatically save photos to the cloud.

3. **Sync music with Groove Music**: Essentially sending yourself a phone-specific link to download the Groove Music app, which will stream music from the OneDrive music folder.

4. **Sync up OneNote to-do lists**: A link to download the OneNote app.

5. Download Office apps for your handset.

6. Get the Outlook app.

7. Download Skype for your handset.

Above: There's a host of options for smartphones, but Windows Mobile devices work the best.

Above: You can download apps like OneNote for any type of handset including iPhone.

USING APPS

INTRODUCTION TO APPS

Apps are all the rage these days, and you'll find them on tablets, smartphones, TVs and even the latest smartwatches. So it's inevitable that Windows 10 will make the most of them too.

Above: Apps dominate the Start menu in Windows 10.

WHAT ARE APPS?

Apps are small programs that help you get things done. They tend to be small and do specific jobs, and there's no one type of app. Unlike traditional Windows programs that you buy in stores, apps are small, lightweight and often free. Their simplicity makes them easy to use, enabling you to dip in and out, getting much more from your computing experience.

Apps are usually operating system specific, so there are dedicated ones for Windows 10 in the same way Apple has apps for its iPhone and iPad devices. Apps for iPad, for example, can't be used on Windows 10, although you'll often see the same titles appearing in the different app stores.

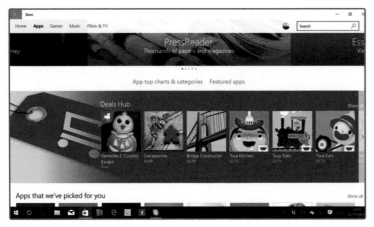

Above: You can download and buy apps in the Windows Store.

Where Do You Download Them?

Every operating system has a marketplace for apps, where you can browse and download. In Windows 10 this is the Windows Store, which you can access from the Start menu. The Windows Store is a one-stop shop for every Windows 10 app, and free and paid-for apps are thrown in together for you to browse.

What's the Difference Between Apps and Normal Programs?

Technically, nothing. Any program is essentially an app. However, Windows 10 apps are lightweight and designed for touch screens, so they use the Modern UI (user interface) in Windows 10, rather than older programs, which can be impossible to use on portable-sized screens.

Hot Tip

There's also an online web-based store for the apps in Windows. Just go to https://www.microsoft.com/en-gb/windows/apps-and-games

THE DEFAULT APPS

You'll meet apps as soon as you log into Windows 10 for the first time, and the new Start menu is home to a host of included options. While we've covered most of the essential apps elsewhere in this guide, here's a rundown of the stock Windows 10 apps.

Calculator

One of the most powerful calculator apps you're likely to find, you can not only switch between normal and scientific layout, but also access specialist keypads for calculating energy, speed, power, time – you name it.

Calendar

Clean design brings order to your calendar chaos. You can add pretty much any existing calendar into Windows 10's, whether it's from Apple, Google or Outlook. You can also have multiple calendars in one place. Turn to pages 190–91 for a full guide to the Windows 10 Calendar.

Above: As you might expect, there's a calculator built in.

Camera

Most devices now have at least one camera built in, and this app lets you snap pictures at will. You can toggle between still images and video on the right-hand side of the window, and the space bar will take the shot. Pictures are stored in the Photos app, and you can jump straight to your shot by clicking the tiny preview in the top right of the Camera window.

Hot Tip

If your device has more than one camera, you can flick between them in the Camera app – just look for an icon with a camera surrounded by an arrow.

Left: The Camera app lets you take pictures using your device's built in snapper, or you can buy a USB one.

Films and TV

Essentially Netflix for Windows 10, this app lets you find and watch films on your PC, tablet or Windows smartphone. The Films and TV app is for watching your content, but will whisk you off to the Windows Store to buy titles. If you have non-Windows Store movies or files on your PC, they will be found here.

Groove Music

Groove Music is the music-playing app for Windows 10. It plays your music collection, lets you make and listen to playlists, and will let you play your collection on other devices if you add the songs to OneDrive. You can also pay a monthly charge to stream a huge catalogue of digital music.

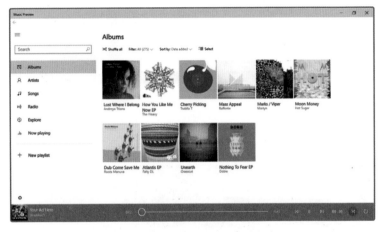

Above: Groove Music enables you to listen to all your music on all your devices.

Mail

The Mail app in Windows 10 is beautifully simple. You can manage multiple accounts simultaneously, including Outlook, Exchange, Gmail, Yahoo, iCloud and any POP3-style account. You can read, reply, organize, tag and file away mail. Turn to pages 138–44 for a full guide.

Maps

Bing Maps is one of the best in the business and quite literally puts the world at your fingertips. You can navigate around the globe using your mouse – or touch

Hot Tip

Maps includes a neat feature called 3D Cities. Select it from the left-hand pane and then select yours from the list. You can then get a 3D feel for the city in amazing detail.

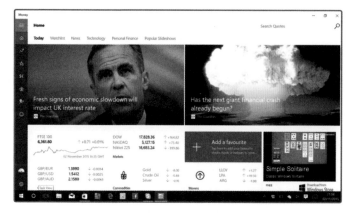

Above: The Money app keeps an eye on your stocks and shares.

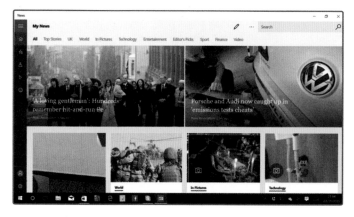

Above: The news app brings the latest headlines, and the Live Tile displays them on the Start menu.

screen if you've got a tablet or hybrid – and pinch and zoom into areas of the map. It also features handy driving directions complete with live traffic.

Money

Essentially a stocks and shares tracking app complete with a news feed for investors, the Money app in Windows 10 also features currency converters and a mortgage calculator.

News

The News app is another stock offering in Windows 10 that's a lot more powerful than it has a right to be. You can sign up for breaking news alerts, opt for local stories as well as international events, and even tailor your news to your interests, such as technology, sports or entertainment.

OneDrive

OneDrive is the online storage app in Windows 10. Every user gets 15GB free to store their files online. This makes your files safe from hardware failures, which is the biggest cause of data loss. In Windows 8 it used to have an interface like other apps, but now it's just listed as a folder within the File Explorer.

OneNote

This app used to be part of Microsoft Office, which isn't included in Windows as standard. OneNote enables you to jot down items, save quick memos and even compile research together. All your notes are saved automatically. Turn to pages 188–89 for a full guide to OneNote.

People

The contacts book for Windows 10 will pull in information from your email accounts as well as social media too. You can add email accounts just like the other apps, but for social media you will need to download the relevant apps from the Windows Store.
If you don't want your entire Twitter following as a contact, you can just turn it off in the Settings menu.

Photos

We go into the nitty-gritty of the Photos app over on pages 194–201 but this is essentially where you can open, view and edit your snaps in Windows 10. You can create and organize albums and even add folders from your OneDrive cloud storage.

Hot Tip
Save any webpage as a OneNote cutting just by clicking the Share button and choosing OneNote.

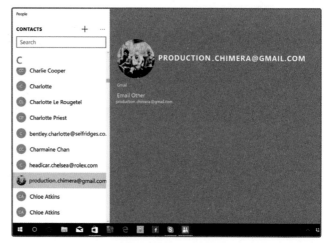

Above: The People app is Windows 10's virtual address book.

Hot Tip
Hit the three little dots next to the Search bar in the People app and choose Settings. You can then tailor your Contacts list. Click Filter contact list to weed out the groups you don't need.

Above: The Photos app is a great way to organize, edit and view your memories.

Phone Companion

An easy way to sync files and music with your existing phone, the Windows 10 Phone Companion app works with Android and iOS handsets as well as Microsoft-based ones.

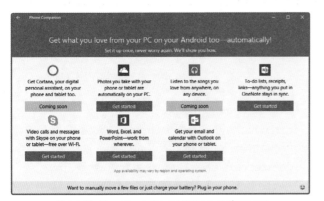

Above: The Phone Companion app helps you configure your smartphone with Windows 10.

It means you can get your snaps from your phone to your PC without any hassle.

Reader

The default app for opening PDFs on your PC, the Reader app lets you search documents, print and make notes. It will also keep your files neatly organized so you can access them through the Reader app, rather than hunting on your PC.

Reading List

An offline viewer for content on your PC, you can save web articles in the Reading List app for later. If you spot something you want to save in Windows Edge, just hit the Share button and then choose Reading List. It will be there when you need it.

Skype

Not actually default in Windows 10, there's an option to Get Skype in the apps list. Skype is Microsoft's ubiquitous messaging and video calling app. It enables you to maintain a friends list, and do anything from instant messaging to voice and video calls.

Sport

The go-to app for sports fans, it's essentially a news feed for fans of any beautiful game. The left-hand bar shows a list of popular sports you can jump to, and you can search for

Hot Tip

You can create themed groups in the Reading List app, so you can keep things organized. Just right-click to bring up an options menu for creating new categories.

Right: Reader lets you view PDF files quickly and easily.

9/17/2015   Itinerary: Dublin

Expedia.co.uk

Dublin
2 Nov 2015 - 4 Nov 2015 | Itinerary # 7136714430673

E-Ticket   *This page can be used as an E-Ticket.*   Itinerary # 7136714430673

Before travelling, print a copy of your itinerary and take it with you!

Important Information

- To manage your booking or check in online (where available) please visit our Manage my Flight page, select your airline and use the booking reference provided below.
- Your return flight consists of two one-way fares which are subject to their own rules and restrictions. If one of your flights is changed or cancelled, it will not automatically change the other flight. You may incur a penalty fee for each flight for additional itinerary changes.
- Proof of citizenship is required for international travel. Be sure to bring all necessary documentation (e.g. passport, visa, transit permit). To learn more, visit our Visa and Passport page . For local destination and health advice, check the Foreign and Commonwealth Office website .
- If your plans change and you need to change or cancel your booking (subject to the applicable Rules & Restrictions below) please call us at 0203 6840237

Total Price

London to Dublin	£231.42
Dublin to London	£137.10
Total Price	**£368.52**

All prices include taxes & fees and are quoted in British pounds sterling. Your two one-way fares may be processed through multiple transactions.

London (LCY) → Dublin (DUB)
2 Nov 2015 - 2 Nov 2015 , 3 one way tickets

CONFIRMED
British Airways   3ANLNF
Expedia.co.uk   3ANLNF
Booking ID

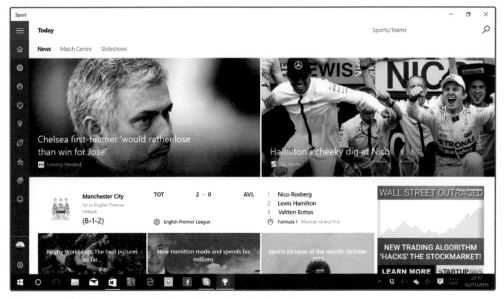

Above: Sports fans will love the news and headlines in the dedicated Windows 10 app.

your favourite teams in the box located in the top right. If you 'star' that team, relevant news and results will populate the main screen.

Twitter

New to Windows 10, there's now a Twitter client in the operating system. The Twitter app enables you to check your stream, compose new tweets and quickly jump to trending topics.

Left: You can use Twitter to stay up with news, even if you don't tell the world what you had for lunch.

Weather

Fire up the Weather app and you
can set your default location and
preferences. Just type your town,
city or location into the search box
and hit enter. The screen will now
offer a full five-day forecast with
insane detail on sunrise, moonrise,
humidity and historical data.

The left-hand side bar offers more
information still. You can view
weather maps of your area, even
more historical averages for your
location, and you can even add
more places.

Xbox

Gamers rejoice: if you're an Xbox
owner you can have your account
details piped into the Windows 10
Xbox app. When you open the app
it will find your account details (if
you use the same Microsoft ID).
You can then get an activity feed
of what your friends are up to,
and even play titles on your
Windows devices. Turn to pages
216–25 for a full rundown of
gaming in Windows 10.

Above: The Weather app in Windows 10 is incredibly powerful and detailed.

Hot Tip

**In the Weather app go to Settings
and choose Always detect my location
to have the local weather displayed
wherever you are in the world.**

Above: Xbox gamers will love using the dedicated Windows 10 app as a second screen.

USING THE WINDOWS STORE

The Windows Store is Microsoft's app marketplace, where you can find and download a host of titles for your Windows 10 PC. From Facebook and utilities to games like Asphalt 8, the Windows Store is packed with a mixture of free and paid-for apps – and there's something for everyone.

ACCESSING THE STORE

All apps are found within the Windows Store, which is available on all Windows 10 devices. You can find the link in the Start menu, indicated by a shopping-bag icon. You can also search using Cortana.

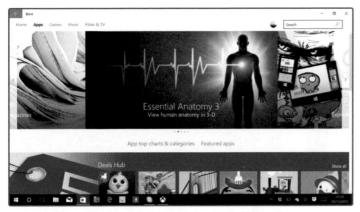

Above: There are thousands of apps to try out in the Windows Store.

Introducing the Store

Once you've entered the Windows Store, you'll be presented with a series of tiles. Highlighted apps are at the top, which are selected by Microsoft as being worthy of your attention. Just keep scrolling down using the mouse or by swiping on a touch-screen device.

Browsing the Store

You'll notice tabs across the top for Apps, Games, Music and Films & TV. In Windows 10 the Store offers more than just apps, and you can buy content to watch on your PC here, too. Tap or click on the apps menu to filter just apps.

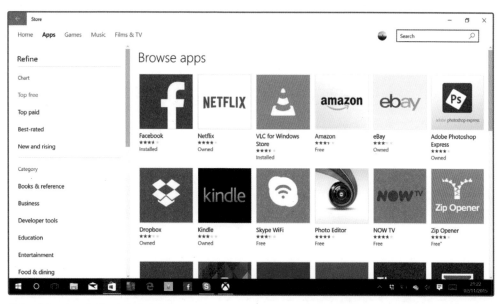

Above: Categories make it easier to find what you need.

Categories

When you're in the Apps or Games sections of the Windows Store you can scroll through Microsoft's suggestions. However, you can drill down quickly into the types of apps you want by tapping or clicking App top charts and categories in the main screen. A new pane will appear on the left-hand side with topics such as entertainment, food, news, weather and more. Tap these for more focused lists of apps.

Charts

In the same window you can get charts of the most popular apps. This is a great way to find

Hot Tip

After the first Spotlight section you'll see apps picked by manufacturers such as Samsung, Sony or Lenovo. Many of these apps will be exclusive to you, and not enjoyed by the wider Windows 10 population. No matter which brand your PC is, the manufacturer's picks will sit second in the list, and while the quality here will be poorer than that of the general Windows Store, it's worth taking a look.

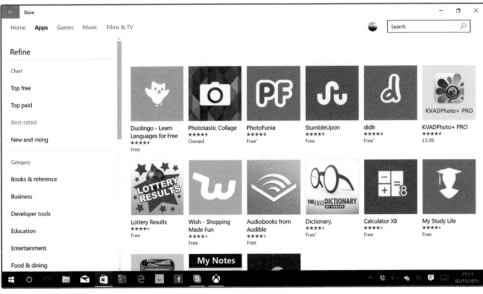

Above: The Charts will help guide you to quality apps.

the best titles and all the essentials will be listed. There's also a chart called New and rising, which helps identify the apps that are gaining popularity.

Free Apps

The Windows Store is a mixture of free and paid-for apps, but no-one really likes forking out when they don't have to. Handily, the Windows Store has a category to let you browse free apps only. Just choose a category from the list and then tap Top free to filter out the complementary apps.

Paid-for Apps

In the main, paid-for apps are better quality than the free ones, for obvious reasons, so if you're

Hot Tip

Each category has sub-sections for new, top paid, top free and a selection of sub-categories. Just tap or click any of these headings to get even more choice, making it easy to find the apps you want.

looking for the best choices, refine your search by clicking or tapping Top paid.

Searching the Store

The search box is located in the top right, and it's easy to just type what you're looking for. Just tap into the box, start typing and the results

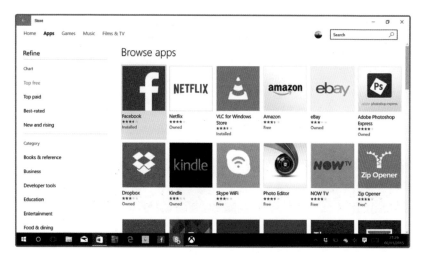

Above: Free and paid-for apps are listed separately.

will appear as you type, narrowing with every stroke. As you see your app appear, just tap or click it to be taken to its page.

Read the Descriptions

Every app has a meaty description, which will tell you what the app does. Just tap or click on any app to bring up the description page. The company that made the app is written underneath the title, and it's worth paying attention to, in case you're about to download a naff knock-off Facebook app.

Games

Apps and games have different stores now, so hit the Games tab at the top of the Apps window to browse the titles on offer. Again, it's well worth looking at the charts by tapping the Game top charts and

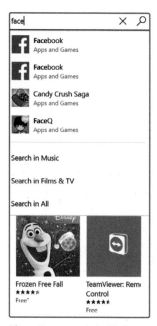

Above: You can search the Windows Store for the apps you want.

Above: There's a whole section of app games for Windows 10.

Hot Tip
You can use the Windows Store as your own chart show. Just click the music tab and then scroll down to a list of the top downloaded tunes.

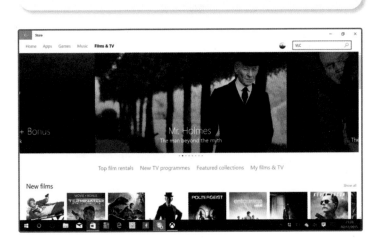

categories option, and then filtering by free games. Be aware that free games in Windows 10 tend to have adverts.

Music
The Windows Store now has a dedicated music shop too. Just click or tap the Music tab at the top of the window. You can buy songs and albums, or subscribe with a Groove Music Pass to listen to as much as you like for a monthly fee.

Films and TV Shows
The Films and TV portion of the store enables you to rent and buy shows to watch on your Windows PC. They can also be streamed to an Xbox on the same network.

Left: Windows Store has its own films section where you can rent and buy titles to watch on your devices.

DOWNLOADING APPS

Just like anything you buy, it's important to make sure you're getting a quality product. The Windows Store is packed with reviews and ratings, as well as ways to manage your downloads so that you're always in control.

BUYING APPS

Like any marketplace the Windows Store offers apps for sale, as well as freebies. These apps are often better quality, can help your PC do incredible things, and most cost less than a pint of beer.

Do Your Research

Before splashing out on an app, it's well worth checking you're buying a quality product. There are refund options available through the Windows Store, but it can be time-consuming, so preventing mistakes is recommended.

Read the Comments

If you scroll even further to the right you can read comments from app users, which

Hot Tip

When you click on an app you can see reviews and recommendations from past users, which can give you a clue about whether your app is worth the cash.

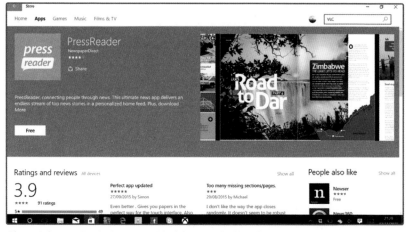

Above: Before you download an app read the fine print to check it's what you're expecting.

Above: Users leave comments on apps, and other people's experiences can be useful before you download.

should give you more information on their thoughts. If you're satisfied, you're ready to download your app.

Check the Fine Print

Below the comments you'll see a list of specs about the app. It's worth casting your eye over the size of the app. By and large Windows 10 apps are very small, but some can be over 200MB, so it's worth considering what you're downloading.

There will also be an age rating for each app (very handy when children want to play games) and the permissions you're allowing the app when you agree to download.

Hot Tip

Once your app has finished downloading it will automatically be installed and added to the Start menu, under 'Recently added' in the left-hand pane. If you can't see it, just tap or click All Apps and then find it in the list.

How to Download an App

Free apps will simply have an install button in the left-hand pane, while paid-for ones will have Buy. To install an app just tap the button and a notification will appear in the top right-hand corner to let you know that the app is installing. Clicking or tapping this will show the download's progress.

Above: Most apps will only take a minute or two to download.

Buying Paid-for Apps

When you press Buy you'll be asked to confirm your account's password before being whisked off to the payment page. You'll need to enter card details, which will be saved for next time.

Check the Progress of a Download

Most apps in Windows 10 will install within a minute or so, but some of the bigger versions such as Microsoft Office or a big Windows 10 update could take hours. If an app is taking its sweet time, just click your account picture in Windows Store and choose Downloads and updates. You should see it listed, complete with a progress bar.

Above: You'll need to set up payment details to buy paid-for apps.

MANAGING YOUR PAYMENTS

When you're spending money it's good to have peace of mind, and Windows 10 puts you in full control. To manage payments on your Windows Store account, go to the Start screen, and tap or click Store to open the Windows Store. Swipe down from the top edge of the screen, then tap Your account.

Tap or click Add payment method or Edit payment method, edit any necessary info, then tap or click Submit.

Add a Payment Method From Your Account

You can download free apps without inputting any payment into Windows 10, but to buy paid-for ones, you'll need to add a credit card. Here's how.

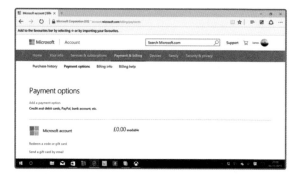

Above: The Windows Store is a safe and secure way for payments and is managed via Microsoft's online system.

1. In the Windows Store click your account picture next to the search box.

2. Choose Payment options from the list.

3. A new web page opens. Sign in with your Windows ID.

4. In the Payment options tab click Add a payment.

5. Enter your banking details.

6. Click Submit.

View Your Billing History

1. In the Windows Store click your account picture next to the search box.

2. Choose Purchased from the list.

Above: You can check your billing history to get a list of paid-for apps.

3. Sign in using your Windows ID.

4. In the Purchase history tab you can see your transactions.

5. Go back in time by using the drop-down menu to select the year.

MANAGING APPS

Just because you downloaded an app doesn't mean it's the end of the story. Developers are always making improvements to their apps, and that means you could be missing out on great new features.

UPDATE APPS

Here's how to update your apps. It really is this simple.

1. Click your account picture in the Windows Store.

2. Select Downloads and Updates.

3. Click check for updates.

4. Install any that you see in the list.

Above: New features are added to apps all the time, so keep them updated.

Move Apps

When you download apps you can have them added to the Start menu, taskbar or desktop. First, find your new app in the Start menu > All apps list. Right-click on it to get options to pin it to the Start menu or taskbar. Alternatively you can just drag it to where you want it.

Turn Off Live Tiles

Some apps will feature the same Live Tiles as your default Windows ones. You can right-click any app in your Start menu and click Turn live tile off to have it become static.

Above: You can organize your Start screen by dragging app tiles around.

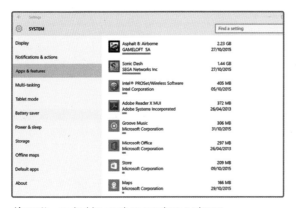

Above: You can check how much space each app is taking up.

See Which Apps are Taking Up the Most Space

Got loads of apps and running out of hard disk space? Well, maybe some of those games you downloaded are taking up more space than you thought. Ask Cortana for Settings and then choose System > Apps and features. This menu will offer a list of every app on your system and its size – and will even put them in order for you.

Configure Default Apps

When you perform certain actions in Windows, like opening a PDF or asking Cortana to send an email, it will be done in a certain app. That's the default app for that action. However, you can choose which apps perform these actions in Windows. Here's how to choose new default programs.

1. Use Cortana to search 'settings' and then choose System.

2. Go to the Default apps option in the left-hand pane.

3. There are different types of action in the main list. Click any to change to a different app, or find a new app in the Windows Store.

4. Any unassigned actions will be represented by a grey box.

5. You can also change the way files are opened by clicking Choose default applications by file type.

6. A bewildering array of file types will be listed. Tap the app or grey box to change the default.

Above: You can force different types of files to use specific apps automatically.

Stop Apps Starting With Windows

If you have an app that's starting up when Windows loads, you can kill that very quickly. Just hit Ctrl + Alt + Delete on your keyboard and then choose Task Manager. You can also just ask Cortana. Click More details and then the Start-up tab. You can right-click any program in this list and choose Disable to make sure it stays closed.

Remove Apps

It's simplicity itself to get rid of Windows 10 apps if you get bored of them. Just right-click any app in the Start menu and choose Uninstall. A new box will appear where you just have to confirm the choice, and the app will disappear from your system as quickly as it arrived.

Right: Banish unwanted apps quickly by right-clicking on a tile and choosing Uninstall.

GET CONNECTED

GET CONNECTED TO THE INTERNET

If you already have an Internet connection set up it's just a case of getting your new Windows 10 PC connected, but if you're setting up your broadband connection for the first time, then you must have the right hardware to connect. Here's what you need.

WHAT DO YOU NEED?

- A subscription to an ISP's broadband service.
- A modem router (supplied by your ISP).
- A PC that has a network adaptor (every modern PC will have this).

For Wireless Connectivity

To connect to your broadband wirelessly you will need:

- A wireless modem router (every modern router will have this).
- PC with a wireless card (all laptops and tablets have one, but check desktop PCs).

Left: Your wireless router is your gateway to the Internet.

Connect to the Internet via Ethernet

After you've signed up to an ISP and you've connected your hardware by following the ISP's instructions, you should be ready to connect to the Internet. Just plug an ethernet cable into the back of the router and then into your Windows 10 PC.

CONNECT TO A WI-FI NETWORK

Wi-Fi isn't just amazingly convenient, it's also the norm. Now laptops and tablets are commonplace, you might not have an ethernet port on your Windows 10 PC at all.

1. The Wi-Fi connection icon is on the taskbar – it looks like the signal icon on your smartphone . If you can't see it, click the up arrow in case it's buried in the list of over-spilling apps.

2. You'll see a list of available networks. Find yours and choose it from the list. Tick the Connect automatically box if you want to have your PC hook up straightaway next time. If you're unsure of the name of your network, it's often written on the side of your supplied router, along with the password.

3. Enter the network security key if you're asked to do so, and then click OK.

A wired internet connection uses an Ethernet cable.

Hot Tip

Got trouble getting a wireless signal across your house? Try investing in a powerline system, which uses two special plugs to send the Internet round your house via the existing electric circuit.

Below: The Wi-Fi connection icon.

Right: Powerline networking can overcome poor signal in your house.

Above: WPS security uses a button to confirm a secure connection.

Hot Tip

As a rule, you should never connect to a network you don't trust, and if you are using public Wi-Fi, never type in information such as usernames or passwords.

Connect via WPS (Wi-Fi Protected Setup)

If your router has a WPS button, you can connect without the hassle of passwords and logins. Turn on the PC and when at the Windows Start screen, go to connect to a network by swiping in from the right edge of the screen, tapping Settings, going to PC Settings and choosing network from the list.

Instead of typing a security key or passphrase, press the Wi-Fi Protected Setup (WPS) button on the router. The router will connect the PC to the network and apply the network's security settings automatically.

WATCH YOUR DATA

If your home Wi-Fi has a data download limit, Windows 10 can help you stick to it. Going over the amount of data allowed by your ISP can be expensive, so Windows has a setting that limits download traffic in the background, so you won't be hit by nasty surprises.

1.   Go to Settings and then Network.

2.   Head to the Wi-Fi tab.

3.   Scroll down to advanced options.

4.   Turn on Set as metered connection.

See What's Eating Your Data

If you still feel like you're using your allowance too frivolously, then you can go to Settings > Network and then choose Data usage. Tap or click Usage details to get an overview of how much data each app has munched through.

CONNECT YOUR PHONE WIRELESSLY

The Connect app is a cool new feature that was brought in with the Windows 10 Anniversary Update, and it lets you connect devices wirelessly, allowing you to broadcast the display of your smartphone or tablet in a window on the Windows 10 desktop. Your Windows 10 device must support Miracast technology for this to work.

To connect your device wirelessly in Windows 10, do the following:

1. Take your Android phone or tablet and pull down the menu (the notification drawer) from the top of the screen. Tap on the Cast or Screen Mirroring icon (often represented as a screen icon with radiating lines in its bottom left corner).

2. A list of devices should appear that you can broadcast your screen on. On your Windows 10 machine, launch the Connect app, and your PC should now appear in the list of devices on your Android phone.

3. Tap the name of your PC and your Android phone will automatically mirror its screen onto your Windows PC, allowing you to control your phone or tablet from the Windows 10 desktop.

Above: Windows 10 will keep an eye on your data usage.

Above: On your Android device, look for the 'Cast' icon to mirror your phone's screen to your Windows PC.

MICROSOFT EDGE EXPLAINED

Microsoft Edge is the name of the new Internet browser in Windows 10. We show you how to get started with mastering this powerful new way to access the web.

GETTING STARTED WITH EDGE

The icon for Microsoft Edge is found on the taskbar, but also within the Start menu. It may look like the old Internet Explorer icon, but this is a brave new world of touch-screen-friendly browsing.

First Steps With Microsoft Edge

When you load Microsoft Edge for the first time you'll see that there's no traditional address bar at the top to type in the website URL. There's a single box in the middle that will act as both a search box and address bar. Just type a web page into it and hit enter.

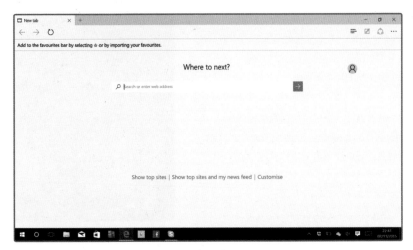

Above: Edge is the new browser in Windows 10.

Browsing

From here browsing using Microsoft Edge is pretty self-explanatory. Just click links to load pages. The address bar now moves back up to the top and is still used for both URLs and searches. Just don't add 'www' if you want to search.

Forward, Back and Refresh

There are some navigation icons in the top left to help you around the web. The back arrow takes you back a page, and the forward arrow onwards a page (if you've already gone back and regret it). The circle icon will reload the page you're on, which is handy if it's being updated live.

Above: The main bar doubles for search terms and URLs.

CUSTOMIZE MICROSOFT EDGE

Microsoft Edge has many ways to customize it to make it your own. It's not just about making it look pretty, it's about using the web more efficiently and getting what you need faster.

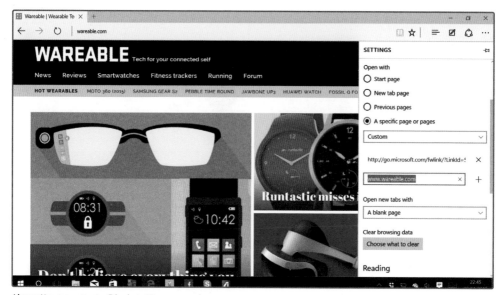

Above: You can customize Edge by setting your own homepage.

Hot Tip

When changing your default homepage you can click the + icon to add multiple tabs when Microsoft Edge loads. The only downside is that opening multiple pages automatically can slow things down, so be picky.

Set a Homepage

By default Microsoft Edge will load up a bunch of news stories from MSN, but you can have anything you like. In Edge click or tap the three little dots in the top right and then choose Settings. Under the Open with header click A specific page or pages. Click the drop-down box and choose Custom, and then type in the web address.

Choose Your Search Engine

Microsoft Edge defaults to search with Bing, which is Microsoft's own search engine. To get Google (or any other search engine) back:

1. Browse to the search engine you want.

2. Go to the right-hand corner menu in Edge and choose Settings.

3. Scroll down to View Advanced Settings.

4. Scroll down again to the Search in the address bar with drop-down box.

5. Click Add new.

6. The browser page you're on will be listed.

7. Choose Add as default.

Above: You can choose which search engine is used by default.

START INPRIVATE BROWSING

Sometimes when you're using your Windows 10 PC you don't want to leave a trail of the websites you've visited. For example, if you're shopping for your partner's birthday present, you might not want to leave it in the history for the Internet's advertising companies to start presenting it to them when they browse.

You can use InPrivate browsing to surf without leaving a trail by opening the browser, clicking the menu button and choosing New InPrivate window.

Hot Tip
You can pin any web page to the Windows 10 Start menu for even faster access. Just click the More actions button on the toolbar and choose Pin to start.

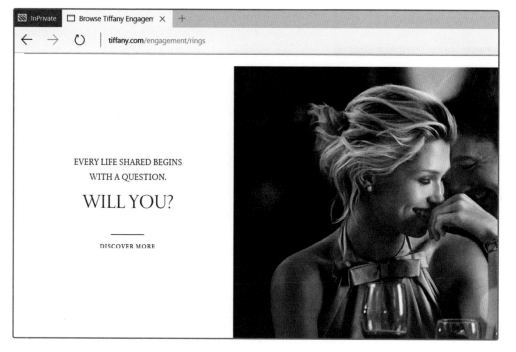

Above: InPrivate browsing lets you surf the web without leaving a history.

FAVOURITES AND BOOKMARKS

We're all creatures of habit and we all have our favourite websites, and that's exactly what the Favourites feature in Microsoft Edge is for. Read on to find out how to bookmark websites.

Above: You can choose to add sites to your Favourites bar.

Above: The Favourites tab stores all your bookmarks.

Add a Website to Your Favourites

Browse to a website you want to bookmark and then click the star icon on the toolbar. You will then get a chance to rename the site for your bookmarks, and strip out a lot of the nonsense that's automatically sucked in.

Organize Your Bookmarks

When you click the Favourites icon to add your bookmark there's a second box to choose where to save it. By default there are two locations, the Favourites list and the Favourites bar.

You can add it to the list uncategorized, or you can create folders within the Favourites list to keep things organized. Click Create new folder and give the new folder a name. Click or tap Add to finish up.

Access Your Favourites

Once you've bookmarked a load of websites it's quick and easy to access them. Just click the Hub icon on the taskbar (three lines) and then choose the favourites tab. All your folders and websites will be listed.

The Favourites Bar

Turned off by default the favourites bar lives at the top of the Microsoft Edge screen, providing quick links to your chosen websites. It has pride of place, so it's for your core sites you use every day. To show the bar, go to Settings and choose Show the favourites bar. To add websites, repeat the steps above, but choose Favourites Bar in the drop-down box.

Clear Your Data

As you browse the web Microsoft Edge will pick up load of information about you – saved passwords, previously visited websites and data within forms. But of course you can clear this quickly and easily.

In the Microsoft Edge settings menu, scroll down to Clear Browsing Data. Click the button and tick what you want to be wiped. If you feel like Edge is collecting too much, go to the Advanced Settings menu. You can prevent the following data being saved by turning off:

- Passwords
- Form entries
- Cookies
- Ads tracking

Above: If you choose to show it, the Favourites bar sits at the top of your screen and can be used for sites you visit every day.

Above: You can clear all the browsing data from Edge in the Settings menu.

MAKE THE WEB EASIER TO READ

The web is full of amazing content but with our busy lives it's not always easy to enjoy it. Microsoft Edge is full of great ways to make the web a better reading experience.

Reading View

Sometimes the websites you want to read don't look very nice – and the problem is getting worse. Pages crowded with adverts, pop-ups and small text can make reading long articles a chore. Any web page can be turned into a luxurious reading experience by clicking the Reading View icon on the taskbar.

Save Content for Later

When you stumble across great but long articles on the web, it's not always convenient to spend half an hour reading them. But it can also be tough to go back and find them later. You can create a Reading List by adding a site to the favourites, clicking on the tab at the top and then choosing Add.

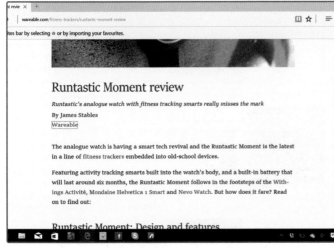

Above: Reading View makes text larger and cleaner for long articles.

Above: Save articles offline to read later using Reading List.

GET CORTANA TO HELP YOU ON THE WEB

Cortana isn't just present on the Windows 10 taskbar, it's also built into Microsoft Edge. You can click on any word on a web page, right-click and choose Ask Cortana. This will offer anything from dictionary definitions to Wikipedia information at the touch of a button.

MAKE EDGE EVEN BETTER WITH EXTENSIONS

The Edge web browser has had a major upgrade with the Windows 10 Anniversary Update and allows you to add plugins (known as 'Extensions') to the browser, making it even more useful.

- **The Amazon Assistant Extension:** Perfect for those of us who love shopping online, as it lets you quickly see the Deal of the Day, compare prices, make Wish Lists and a lot more all from Edge – without having to go to the Amazon website.

- **The LastPass Extension:** This helps Edge store your passwords safely and securely so you can log on easily to your favourite websites in seconds whilst giving you complete peace of mind.

- **Adblock Plus:** This is another essential Extension which blocks annoying ads and tracking cookies from websites you visit. This makes websites look better, they load faster and you're less likely to get any nasty malware from dodgy ads.

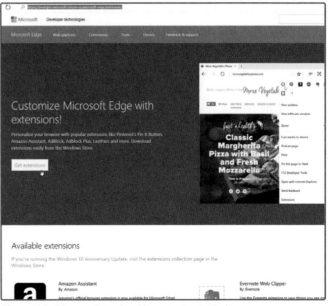

Above: Make Edge even better by adding extensions to the browser.

To browse available Extensions and add them to Edge, click the '•••' icon in the top-right hand corner of Edge and select Extensions > Get extensions from the Store. You can also go to https://developer.microsoft.com/en-us/microsoft-edge/extensions/ to see the Extensions. To choose one you want, click 'Install' and it will be automatically added to Edge.

CHOOSE WHEN TO PLAY FLASH ANIMATIONS

Another welcome new feature in Edge is click-to-play Flash functionality, which means when you land on a page with Flash content it doesn't automatically play. While Flash animations often look good, they are also regularly used for screen-hogging adverts, or blast out loud music when you're peacefully browsing the web.

Flash-heavy websites can take a lot longer to load as well, which is why it's so great that Edge now pauses the Flash videos when the pages load. If you want to play them, simply click on the Flash animation and it will start.

PIN TABS IN EDGE

Thanks to the Windows 10 Anniversary Update you can now make browsing multiple websites at once even easier. Each website is shown in Edge as a tab at the top of the screen, and clicking on a tab brings up the corresponding webpage.

Above: Pin your favourite tabs to make sure they are easily accessible when you're browsing the Internet.

If you end up with a number of websites open at once, this tab bar can become unruly. This is where the ability to pin tabs in Edge comes in. Right-click the tab of a website you want to keep an eye on, such as an important website you're using for work, and select 'Pin tab'. This tab will now appear separate from the others and will not disappear when you shut down Edge. Instead it will still be there when you next launch the Edge browser. This also helps prevent you accidentally closing the tab. If you do want to remove it, right click the tab and select 'Close'.

NOTIFICATIONS IN EDGE

Edge can now display web notifications, so if you've got Whatsapp open in a web page in Edge and someone sends you a message, then Edge will display a notification to alert you. This means you no longer have to install apps – instead just log into the websites and Edge will do the rest!

USING SWIPE GESTURES

Do you browse the Internet with Edge on your tablet? The good news is that it's now easier than ever

Above: Never miss a message again thanks to web notifications in Edge.

thanks to a new update that brings Swipe Gestures to the web browser, making it ideal for reading the web on touchscreen devices. Now if you want to leap back a page when browsing, swipe your finger from left to right.

THE MAIL APP EXPLAINED

The Mail app has been given a good overhaul in Windows 10 to make it one of the most potent email clients around. Built with touch-screen devices in mind, but equally as good for traditional mouse and keyboard users, it's clearly laid out, well-designed and powerful.

SET UP YOUR EMAIL

If you've signed in with your Windows ID, the Mail app will open with your email already present. The Mail app is completely open, so it doesn't matter if you have a Microsoft-based Hotmail or Outlook address, or a Gmail. Whichever email you've

Hot Tip

You can run multiple email accounts simultaneously, making the Mail app perfect for home and business users alike.

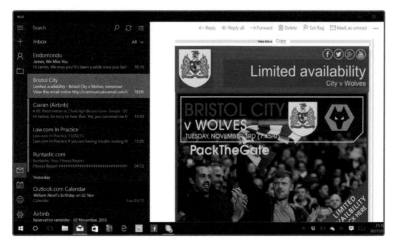

Above: The Mail app is built into Windows 10.

used for your Windows ID will be found as soon as you open the app.

Add Other Accounts

When you open the app for the first time, Windows should prompt you to add any other accounts you have. It's not unusual to have more than one email address, and you can have as many as you like in the Mail app. If Windows doesn't prompt you to add another account it's still easy to set up multiple email addresses.

1. Open the Mail app from the Windows 10 Start menu.

2. Hit the cog icon at the bottom of the left-hand pane.

3. Tap or click Accounts.

4. Tap or click Add an account, choose the type of account you want to add, then add your username and password.

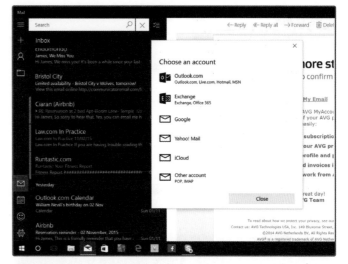

Above: You can have multiple accounts in the Mail app.

USING THE MAIL APP

Once your email is imported into Windows 10, it's time to start sending. The Mail app is really easy to use and puts everything at your fingertips.

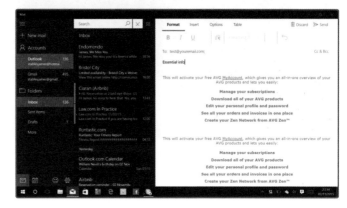

Above: Composing messages in the Mail app is quick and easy.

Write a New Mail

Just click the + New Mail button at the top of the left-hand menu to open a blank message. Type your recipient's email into the 'To' line and then write a subject to help them categorize it.

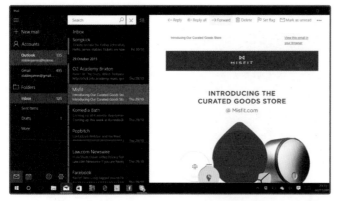

Above: You can reply, reply all and forward messages.

Above: Searching for mail makes it easier to find what you need.

Select Multiple Messages

To select multiple messages, just click the List icon on the top of the inbox pane. Messages in the inbox will then have a small square appear. Check these boxes to mark emails, so you can perform batch tasks like deleting or moving.

Reply, Reply All or Forward

Open an email and it will be previewed in the right-hand pane. A menu of options will appear at the top, letting you reply, reply all (which goes to all recipients in the original email) or forward the message to someone else.

Delete Messages

Select one or more messages and then tap or click the Delete icon in the top of the middle or right-hand pane.

Search for Messages

You can quickly find someone's name or text from an email message by tapping or clicking the Search icon.

Print a Message

Select an email message and then click the three little dots at the top of the right-hand pane. In the new drop-down menu choose Print. A new window will appear to change the settings.

Send Attachments

In a new email message, tap or click Insert followed by Attach on the menu bar. Select the file you want to add to the message, and then tap or click Attach. You can also attach multiple files.

Add a Cc/Bcc

Adding a third person into an email is called a Cc, and you can add these in a new message window by clicking the link on the 'To' line. A Bcc (blind cc) means that the extra person you add won't be visible to the other recipient(s).

Mark Messages as Read/Unread

Select one or more messages, then swipe down from the top of the screen and choose Flag, Junk or Mark unread.

Above: You can quickly add files to your emails, but don't let them get too big.

View Folders

Click on any of your accounts and a list of folders will appear underneath. These will feature standard entries like the inbox, sent items and junk mail folders, but also any you've created for storing emails. You can't create or edit folders in the Mail app – you'll have to go to your main webmail for that.

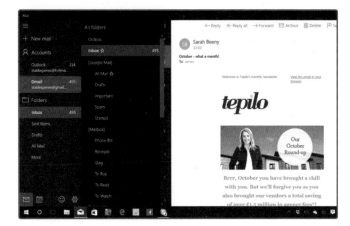

Above: Folders are a great way to organize email.

Move to a Folder

You can send any email to a folder by clicking on the message and then choosing Move from the extra options drop-down. A list of folders will appear from the left for you to select.

Above: Add any email sender to your contacts.

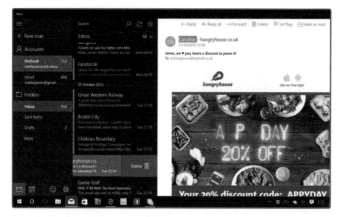

Above: Swiping is a quick and easy way to deal with mail, such as deleting messages.

Add a Contact

Tap or click an email address from an email to create a new entry in the People app. Tap or click the Save icon in the top-right corner.

MAIL YOUR WAY

Now you've got your mail working, it's time to start making it easier to manage. In this day and age it's easy to get swamped by your inbox, so let's get it back under control.

Use Gestures

If you're using a touch-screen PC you can take advantage of a host of gestures and swipes that make dealing with emails faster. By default these gestures are:

- **Swipe left:** Delete an email.
- **Swipe right:** Flag and email for later.
- **Long press:** Get more options.

Change Gestures

As with most Windows apps the gestures in Mail are completely customizable. Just hit the Settings menu via the cog at the bottom of the left pane and then choose Options. You can change the action of a left and right swipe in the drop-down menus.

Add a Signature

You can have a customized signature added automatically at the end of an email, to add that professional touch. It could be your job title, contact details or just a witty little sign-off. In the Options menu scroll down to Signature and type your own instead of the bog standard 'Sent from Mail for Windows 10'. Or you can turn it off altogether.

Reorganize Your Mail

Everyone's brains work differently, and you should have a say in the way you organize your mail. By default the Mail app will stack conversations, which means that multiple messages will be grouped together. However, some people just like all emails to appear in the order they arrive: to have it that way, turn off Show messages arranged by conversation in the Options menu.

Don't Get Bugged By Email

If new messages are taking over your Action Centre then you can turn them off. In the Options menu again, just scroll to the bottom and turn off Show in Action Centre.

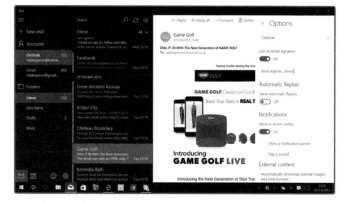

Above: Add a signature to the bottom of your email to save time and add a professional touch.

MESSAGING AND SKYPE

Windows 10 isn't just a stuffy old operating system for running apps and surfing the web; it also brings you closer to your friends and family. Microsoft owns Skype, one of the biggest names in web video calling, and it's integrated the service into native Windows 10 apps as well as its own desktop apps.

MESSAGING

The Messaging app in Windows 10 is like a built-in instant messenger, which is increasingly replacing text messages as the best way to chat with friends and family. This kind of messaging has long been a feature of the desktop Skype app, but it's it's now built into the universal Messaging app, which can be used across PCs, tablets and phones.

Above: Skype video calling and its Messaging app is now fully integrated across all Windows 10 devices.

Sign In

You can fire up the Messaging app by searching in Cortana. When it loads for the first time, it will ask you to sign in with your Microsoft ID. If you already have a Skype ID and it's different to your Windows login, enter that instead.

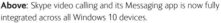

Right: Sign into the Messaging app with your Microsoft ID or Skype ID.

Search Contacts

Once you're logged in you will see the main Messaging screen. If you've used Skype before, then this will be auto-populated with your latest chat conversations. To start a new conversation, just tap or click the + icon and then start typing the name of a contact.

Send Messages

Once you choose a contact, a blank chat window will appear on the right-hand side of the Skype window. Type your message into the bottom box and press enter to send. The message will appear in the main window, and when your contact replies, that will appear underneath.

Attach Files

You can also send files such as documents or photos. To send one from within the chat, just click the paperclip icon next to the message box and then choose your document from the list. If someone sends you a file, it will appear in the chat window. Just tap to download.

Hot Tip

Sometimes chats can be annoying if you're busy. Just click the three dots on the toolbar to the right-hand side and then click Mute to not be disturbed by it. To resume the chat, you'll have to remember to unmute.

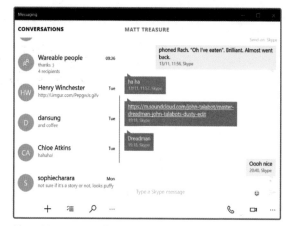

Above: Messaging is just like sending traditional text messages.

Hot Tip

Click the list icon to start editing conversations and then check the boxes of any chats you want to end. Then just click or tap the bin icon to have them deleted.

Above: Video calling brings you closer to your friends and family.

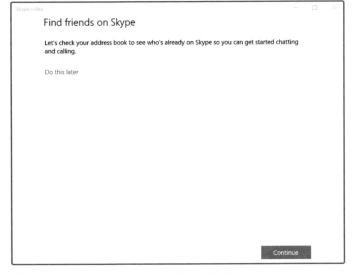

Above: Skype can automatically access your address book to locate people who are already on Skype whom you may wish to video call.

SKYPE + VIDEO

Skype is synonymous with video and now it gets a dedicated Windows 10 universal app. You can use it to video chat with friends and family, which is a great way of getting closer to the people you love. We show you how to get started.

Set Up and Find Friends

Fire up the app by searching for 'skype video' in Cortana. When it starts it will prompt you to add any contacts to Skype that you already have. However, you can skip this step and go straight into the app.

Find Your Existing Contacts

If you have existing Skype contacts, you can see them by clicking the icon with two figures at the top of the window. Choose a contact from the list and then you will see options for calling. Choose Skype Video and the call will start automatically.

Add a New Video Contact

If you don't already have Skype contacts, then click the icon with a person and a plus. A new box will open which will let you search for a contact. You can write their full name, Skype name or email. When you see your contact, click to call them.

PHONE APP

Windows 10 completes a trio of universal communication apps with the new Phone app. This enables you to make voice calls from within Windows 10, which can save you money and saves your mobile plan minutes – especially when calling overseas.

Make a Voice Call

The Phone app in Windows 10 is far simpler than the desktop version of Skype or the Skype Video app. Just search 'phone' and choose it from the list in Cortana. When it opens you'll get a blank window. Click the people icon at the bottom to search for a contact.

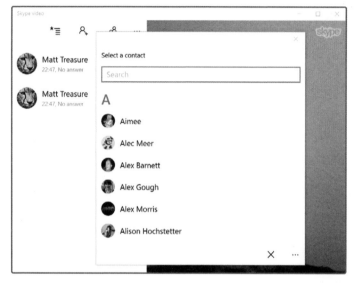

Above: It's easy to find contacts you already have in Skype.

Above: It's also easy to search for contacts manually to add them to your Skype contacts and call them.

Create a Speed Dial List

You can create a sort of phonebook in the Windows 10 Phone app. Just tap the speed dial menu icon at the top and then the plus that appears at the bottom of that menu. Choose a friend to put them on speed dial.

> ## Hot Tip
> **Most PCs have built-in cameras now, but if yours doesn't you'll need to invest in a USB one.**

THE NEW SKYPE APP

With the arrival of the Windows 10 Anniversary Update, the Skype app has been redesigned, integrating it further into Windows 10, and making it work seamlessly with the latest version of Microsoft's operating system. The new Skype app has had a facelift, and it now has a dark theme that ties in with the look of Windows 10 (though you can change to a brighter Light Theme in the Skype app's settings).

To launch the new Skype app, make sure you have the Windows 10 Anniversary Update installed, then open up the Start menu and look for either 'Skype' or 'Skype Preview'.

Above: The Skype app encompasses text messaging, video and phone calls in one powerful app.

In the new version of Skype you can access features by pressing the Menu icon, which is represented by three horizontal lines. The menu that appears gives you quick access to recent conversations, contacts and bots. Bots are a new feature of Skype that let you talk to automated accounts run by computers that can be interacted with as if they were human!

Start a Voice Call

Starting a voice call is easy. Just click a contact's name from the left-hand pane and then click the phone icon. The call will then start.

Video Chat

Starting a video call is much the same as a voice call. Choose a contact and click the video icon. You can also add people to the conversation by pressing the icon to the right.

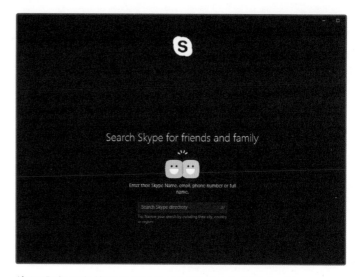

Above: Finding and adding contacts to Skype is easier than ever in Windows 10.

Call Landlines

One final trick up Skype's sleeve is the ability to call landline numbers. It's a great way to cheaply call overseas numbers and annoying chargeable business numbers and hotlines. You can access the dialler by clicking the Call phones icon under your Skype picture. You will need to add some credit to your account, which can be done by clicking Add Skype Credit in the right-hand pane. You can then dial a number just like a normal telephone.

Above: You can call landlines via Skype if you add some credit to your account.

Hot Tip

Calls don't have to be one-to-one as they are on your landline. You can add groups of people to create conference calls.

MAPS APP

The Windows 10 maps app uses Microsoft's own Bing service for some pretty impressive features. Aside from just finding your way, the Maps app can also provide directions, traffic information and more.

VIEWING WINDOWS 10 MAPS

When you load the app for the first time, you'll see a map in the main screen. Using your IP address your PC knows vaguely where you are, so it should centre over your approximate location.

Move the Map

You can drag the map around and it will load up as you scroll. You can also zoom in and out. You can do this by clicking the plus and minus icons in the right-hand tool strip or by pinching

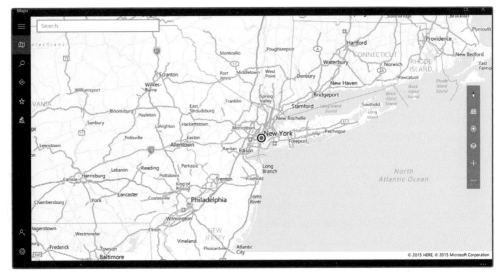

Above: The Maps app lets you zoom around the world.

and zooming on your touch screen or mouse trackpad. You can also rotate the map by placing two fingers on the screen and twisting them in a circular motion.

Above: You can tilt the angle to get a better view.

Toolbar on the Right

The Windows 10 Maps app features a neat toolbar on the right-hand side, which is filled with useful tools:

- **Rotate map**: For those without the luxury of touch screens, the top icon lets you rotate the map. Click the icon to align it north or use the two buttons that extend out to rotate clockwise or anti-clockwise.

- **Tilt**: You can change the map's perspective with the three tilt options, which give you a better view of the area you're studying.

- **Show my location**: Click this and the Maps app will zoom into your exact spot and place a handy blue dot for good measure.

- **Choose view**: You can switch between the default road view and aerial photography, and turn traffic on and off from here.

- **Zoom**: Zoom in and out with the plus and minus icons.

Above: Maps also uses aerial photography.

Above: You can get down to street level using Streetside View.

Streetside View

Streetside is Microsoft's version of Google Streetview and enables you to take a virtual walk down any street, which gives you a much better feel of the area. To turn it on just choose map view and turn on Streetside. Now just double-click or tap on any street to dive in.

SEARCH

The second tab in the left-hand menu is for search, although there's a handy box in the top left which is always on hand.

Get Full Information

You can search in Windows 10 for a place, country, city or any landmark. The screen will now split in two, showing the map view on the right and more detailed information on the left. You get:

- **The address**: There's a directions link, which opens a new menu with a host of different options for travel.

- **Streetside view preview**: Click the window to get a full Streetside view, which you can navigate.

- **Sharing options**: You can star the location to have it saved on the map, share by email, messaging or social media, and pin it to the Start menu.

- **Ideas for nearby restaurants, attractions and amenities**: Click any to have them plotted on the map.

DIRECTIONS

One of the Windows 10 Map app's best features is its ability to give directions. You can search a location and then click for directions or just head to the tab to get started.

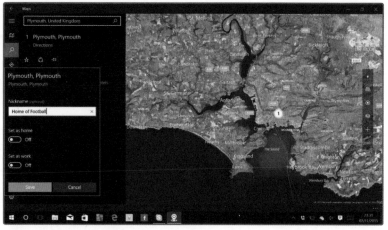

Above: Search for places or businesses and then save them for later.

Find a Route

When you open the Directions tab there are two boxes to fill out: your start point and your destination. By default the start point will be set to your current location, so change this if you're simply planning head. Type your destination in, using a name, place or postcode.

Above: You can get directions for your journey in Maps and use your device as a satnav.

Choose How to Get There

By default the Maps app will offer driving directions, but you can also compare routes for public transport and walking. The options to switch are found at the top of the left pane. Just click an icon for new directions.

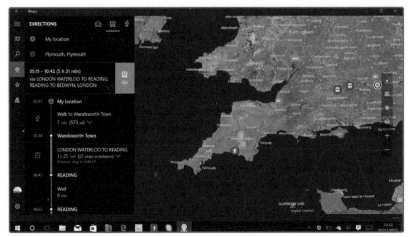

Above: Directions includes details for public transport too.

Choose the Best

You'll get multiple directions for each journey, so you can choose which suits you. As you click them from the list, the route will be shown on the map over on the right.

Head on Out

When you're set you can press Go, which effectively turns your PC into a satnav. This is great for Windows 10 Mobile devices, so you can use it in your car.

Change the Units of Measurement

If you want to change the units of measurement in the Maps app it's easy. Just head to the Settings menu by clicking the gear icon and then switch between imperial and metric.

Change Preferred Direction Type

If you don't own a car it can get a little tiresome that Windows 10 continually offers driving directions. Again, in the Settings menu, you can change the default directions to your preferred mode of transport.

FAVOURITES

Just like web pages you can set favourite places in the Maps app so you're not constantly searching for the same places. Here's how.

Set a Home

You can set a home and work location so it's easier to check traffic and journey times. Just search a location and then hit the Favourite icon in the results. In the new window you can give the place a nickname and tag it as either work or home.

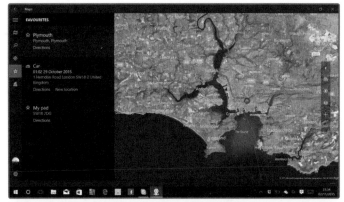

Above: Pin locations as favourites to find them more easily next time.

Find Your Favourite Places

Each will now be listed in the Favourite places tab in the Maps app. When you're searching for directions you can also use the nickname instead of the exact address, for example home, my pad, mum's house etc.

3D CITIES

The final option is the 3D Cities tab. The Maps app has listed some of the most popular cities, where

Above: 3D Cities lets you explore places from your armchair.

the whole place can be accessed through a rich 3D render. You can also change the viewing angle by using the overlaid controls present on the right side of the Maps app.

Using 3D Cities

3D Cities works exactly the same as the normal mapping. You can drag and zoom around, explore the city and change views using the right-hand toolbar. It's not that useful, but good fun and a nice way to get a feel for cities from the comfort of your PC.

SOCIAL MEDIA

Social media apps are a mainstay of any operating system and Windows 10 is no different. While there's a bit of a dearth of apps beyond Twitter and Facebook, integration for social media is baked right into the operating system.

Above: Facebook is the biggest social network and has its own Windows 10 app.

Above: Search for friends in order to connect with them.

FACEBOOK

Facebook is the daddy of social networks and as you'd expect there's a fully fledged app from the Windows Store. It doesn't do any more than the web version, but by choosing the app you enable masses of integration from within Windows 10. To get started, just download the app from the Windows Store.

Add Friends

You'll need a Facebook account to get started, which you can sort out over at www.facebook.com, then use your username and password to sign into the Windows 10 app. Once in the app you can search for friends in the top-left box, and click on their name to view their profile. From there you can click Add Friend, which they will need to accept.

Stay Up With the News

When you have friends added in Facebook you'll see their activity, statuses, photos and more in the main Timeline – the central window in the Facebook app. Click to view photos and you can register your approval using the Like button.

Add Photos in Facebook

Of course you can upload your own things for your friends to look at. You can write a status by clicking on the News Feed tab on the left and clicking Status. You can also add photos: click Photos on the same tab and then Choose from library. Choose photos from the next window and choose Select images to upload followed by Post.

Stay Up With Events

One of the best things about Facebook is the way you can invite friends to gatherings and parties. You can't create events in the Windows 10 app, but you can view ones you've been invited to, as well as post on the wall and see who's going.

Above: Your friends feed dominates the app's screen.

Hot Tip

Choose multiple photos by holding Ctrl on your keyboard as you click.

Above: You can view events and invitations in the Facebook app.

Notifications

When you get notifications in Facebook you'll see them in the top-right corner. A number will appear on the Notifications icon when there's something for your attention. However, you'll also see them in the Action Centre. Just swipe in from the right in Windows 10 or click the icon in the tray to get a list of any recent notifications.

Hot Tip

You can set your Facebook account picture to be the same as your Windows 10 one using Profile Sync. You'll be prompted when you first install the Facebook app. However, you can do it later by clicking the menu button on the far left of the Facebook app title bar and then choosing Profile Sync.

TWITTER APP

The Twitter app comes built into Windows 10, and is a great way to keep up with the news in your feed, check your mentions or send direct messages. To access it, just look in the All Apps section of the Start menu or ask Cortana for Twitter.

Above: Twitter is a powerful real-time social network.

Send a Tweet

To add your own tweet to the mix just click the quill icon at the bottom of the left-hand menu. In the new box type your message: keep it below 140 characters; you can add a picture, however. Just tap or click the Photo icon and choose one from your PC.

Timeline

The main screen of the Twitter app is filled with the tweets from people or organizations you follow in chronological order. If you're yet to follow anyone, then you'll need to head to the search button in the bottom-left and find some people.

Trending

The beauty of Twitter is how instantaneous it is, and that's where the Trending tab comes in. Click the icon for a list of topics the world is talking about. Click a topic for a stream of people's tweets.

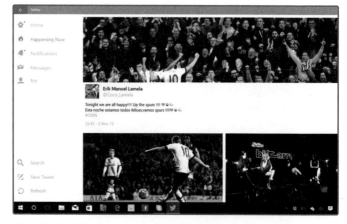

Above: Check out Trending to see what the world is talking about.

Notifications

Notifications in Twitter can consist of people mentioning you, retweeting or favouriting your tweets or following you. You can check these by clicking the button with the bell icon in the left-hand panel.

Search

Twitter is increasingly being used as a search engine as it's such a great source of real-time information. Aside from finding people to follow, you can search for anything, from news stories to what the queue is like outside your local museum.

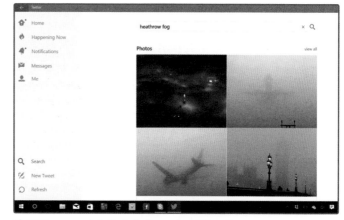

Above: You can search Twitter to find keywords and information.

SOCIAL MEDIA AND THE ACTION CENTRE

As we've mentioned, the Action Centre brings notifications from all your social media apps and puts them into one place. This makes it easy to keep on top of what's going on and means you don't have to keep diving into apps. The Action Centre can be summoned by swiping from the right-hand side or clicking the icon in the tray.

Managing Your Action Centre

Your feed can quickly become filled with social media notifications, so you can use the Action Centre to keep on top. The down arrow will expand a notification in full, so you can read mentions and direct messages. The X icon will dismiss it. You can click to open the message in the relevant app, or alternatively remove it from your Action Centre.

SHARING IN WINDOWS 10

A handy part of Windows 10 is the way you can share information between apps quickly and easily, using the built-in share tool. In any app – for example Photos – you can select an item you want to share and then hit the Share button. Your social media apps will be in the list. When you choose them the relevant app will fire up and your item will be ready to post.

Above: Facebook and Twitter notifications will arrive in the Action Centre.

Above: You can rid the Action Centre of notifications by pressing the X.

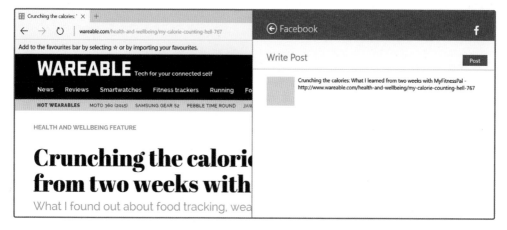

Above: Social apps appear in the baked-in Sharing tool in Windows 10, to make uploading pictures easier.

GET ORGANIZED

ACCESS YOUR FILES IN WINDOWS 10

Our digital lives are full of files. Work documents, holiday snaps, internet shopping receipts, holiday itineraries – and they all reside on our PCs. When it comes to finding, organizing and retrieving your files, File Explorer is your friend. It's been a mainstay of Windows for decades but in Windows 10 it's even more useful.

MASTERING FILE EXPLORER

File Explorer is where you explore the trees of folders and files that make up your PC. You can access any folder on your hard drive here, even the ones that hold the critical system files. You can find the File Explorer icon on the Windows 10 taskbar. It also has a permanent spot on the Start menu.

File Explorer is the best way to view your documents, pictures and files.

File Explorer Explained

1 Quick access
The left-hand pane is a customizable list of folders, so it's easy to get to the ones you want. Just drag any folder into the left pane to have it pinned there.

2 Ribbon
When you click the Home, Share or View button you will see the Ribbon, which is full of options for organizing and editing your files.

Hot Tip
You can make the Ribbon stay permanently by going to the View tab, right-clicking Preview Pane and then choosing Maximize the Ribbon.

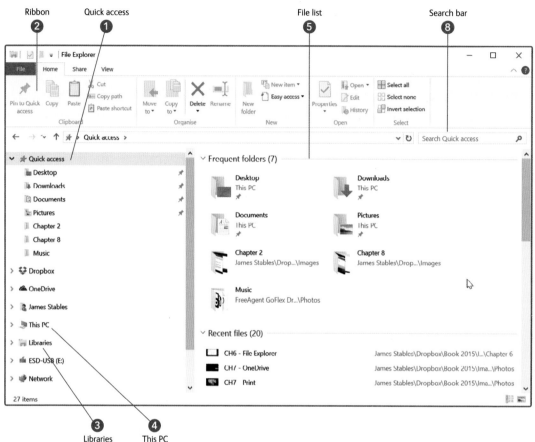

3 Libraries

Libraries are folders for storing your most used files, divided into common types. You can also link folders to a library, even if they exist elsewhere, so they're easier to find.

4 This PC

Delve beyond the libraries in This PC and you will find the structure of your PC's hard drive. Your hard drive is commonly labelled C: and is a giant folder that contains all the critical files that make your PC tick.

5 **File list**

The main window is the file list. Click any folder in the left pane, and double-click to open files or folders in the main window. You can change the way your files appear in the View Ribbon, choosing between icons, lists and extra details.

6 **Column headings (see picture opposite bottom)**

When your files are in a list, column heads appear. You can click them to sort the list into order, and click them again to sort the other way, for example A–Z and Z–A.

7 **Details/Preview pane**

It's turned off by default but you can open a pane on the right to see previews of your files. Just go to View and then click Preview Pane.

8 **Search bar**

You can search within files using the bar in the top right. Tap or click Search tools, which appears in the top bar. You can save the search for quicker access next time.

9 **Media controls**

If you're browsing a folder of pictures or video, a new tab will appear at the top, enabling you to preview video or start a picture slideshow straight from File Explorer.

7 Preview pane

Right: The Ribbon is an enhanced menu bar with multiple tabs.

ORGANIZE YOUR FILES

While Windows 10 may look all orderly now, after a few months of good use you'll find it brimming with photos, files and documents from your everyday life. Here's how to stay organized.

Change Views

In the main pane you'll see all the files contained within the selected folder. However, how those files appear is completely up to you. In the View tab on File Explorer you can choose a bunch of different modes for your icons. You can have them displayed as Extra Large icons, which become mini-previews, all the way down to a list with details such as filename, size, type and date modified. You can sort these by clicking the headers.

Above: You can change the icons between large previews and detailed lists.

⑥ Column headings

Above: You can sort columns by different details.

Hot Tip

Windows key + E will open a File Explorer window in seconds, without having to even touch your mouse.

Above: The libraries make organizing your files easier.

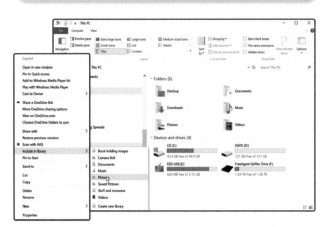

Above: You can make any folder a Windows library.

Use the Predetermined Libraries

Windows 10 comes with a bunch of libraries for your documents already in place, so use them. In File Explorer you will find libraries for documents, music, pictures and videos, which covers most data types. In any library you can create a folder by right-clicking and choosing New > Folder.

Add Folders to Libraries

While libraries are physical folders for storing files, they're also hubs for content stored anywhere on your PC. Add any existing folder to a library really quickly. Just right-click a folder and choose Add to library, and it will appear within the list, even if the folder is located elsewhere.

Make Any Folder a Library

You can make a new library if you feel that Windows 10's libraries don't cover your

---

Hot Tip

Only see libraries in the left-hand pane by going to the View tab, and then selecting Navigation pane > Show libraries.

needs. If you need a home for your receipts, for example, and you don't want to use the Documents library, just right-click the folder, go to Include in library and then choose Create New Library.

Pin a Folder to Quick Access

Quick Access puts your libraries right at the top, making it easier to find what you need. But again, you can pin any folder there to save clicking through sub-folders. Just right-click any folder and choose Pin to Quick Access. Handy if you use certain folders a lot.

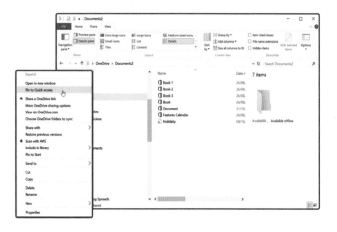

Above: You can pin any folder to the Quick Access tab.

Tag and Star Images

Images tend to be the toughest kind of files to organize, as a folder of holiday snaps can run into hundreds of very similarly named items. In a folder of images in Windows 10 just choose View > Details Pane. Click any image and then add tags or star ratings to individual files. You can then ask Cortana for 'pictures of mum' and it will return results based on your tags.

Above: Pictures can be tagged and given star ratings, so you can find people, events or your favourite snaps faster.

ONEDRIVE

Since the Anniversary Update, Windows 10 now comes with 5GB of cloud storage, which is handy for keeping files online so you can access them from anywhere. It also makes for a safe back-up, away from the dangers of disk crashes or damage. We show you just how it works.

Above: OneDrive is Microsoft's cloud storage service.

Above: You get 5GB of free online storage.

ONEDRIVE ON YOUR PC

In Windows 8 OneDrive was a slightly limited app within the Start screen, but in Windows 10 it's built into the operating system so seamlessly that you'd be forgiven for missing it.

What Is OneDrive?

OneDrive is Microsoft's own 'cloud storage' service, which essentially means a hard drive stored on the Internet, accessed via your Windows ID. When you use an email address to sign into Windows 10, you automatically get 5GB of storage – which is a generous amount for free.

Why Use OneDrive?

When you store files on OneDrive you can access them from anywhere, on any

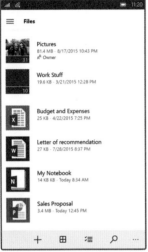

Above: OneDrive enables you to access files on any device.

device. That means your files can be reached on your phone, on your tablet or even from an Internet café in the wilds of Borneo. What's more, your data is safe from hard disk crashes or your PC being stolen, so it's a lot more secure.

Finding Your OneDrive Folders

There's no OneDrive app in Windows 10, and the folders appear along with your hard drive files in File Explorer. They behave exactly like any other folder on your PC, except when you add files to them they're also copied to your online account. You can manage those online folders just as you would your Documents library online.

Adding Files to OneDrive

You can just drag and drop any file or folder to OneDrive and have it saved there. Alternatively, if you're saving a file, you can just set the location to OneDrive as you would for any local folder.

Offline Access

By default any OneDrive folder is also stored on your PC, giving you two copies. That means you can work with those files even if you don't have an Internet connection. When you get back online, the newly edited file stored locally on your PC will be synced with your online storage, so they match up.

Above: You can organize and view files just as you would any other folder.

Choose OneDrive Folders to Sync

All your OneDrive folders will sync with your Windows 10 PC, and will appear in File Explorer. However, you can exclude folders you don't want to see in Windows 10 very easily.

1. Find the OneDrive icon in your notification area in the bottom right.

2. Right-click and choose Settings.

3. Go to the Choose folders tab and then hit the Choose folder.

4. All your OneDrive folders will be listed; untick any you don't want on your PC.

5. Press OK to apply the changes.

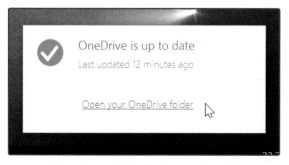

Above: You can check OneDrive's status in the notification area.

Search OneDrive Folders

OneDrive folders are searchable just like your locally stored ones. If you use Cortana to search for the filename, it will appear in the list along with other files.

OneDrive Folder Status

In Windows 10 File Explorer you will notice tiny icons next to the OneDrive folders. A green tick means that the folder has synced with the web and both folders are the same. Two arrows forming a circle means that your PC is currently copying that set of files to the web, but at the moment the two aren't synced. A red cross means that the two are out of sync and a problem means the sync cannot occur.

> ## Hot Tip
> You can buy more storage to expand OneDrive beyond 5GB: 50GB is just £1.99/$1.99 a month.

ONEDRIVE ON THE WEB

To log into OneDrive just browse to http://onedrive.live.com. You'll be prompted to sign in with your Microsoft ID, which should be the same one you use to log into your Windows 10 PC.

Access Files and Folders

The files and folders you've saved from your Windows 10 PC appear in the main window, and can be found by pressing the Files tab in the left-hand pane. Just single-click to access a folder.

View Photos

Most documents and photos can be viewed on the web. Just click a photo to have it open in full view, and if it's a folder full of images, just press the left or right arrow on screen or your device's keyboard to skip through like a slideshow.

Above: You can log into OneDrive from a web browser.

Upload Files and Download Files

You don't have to add files to OneDrive via your Windows 10; you can do it from the browser window should you be away from your main PC. Click to open a folder or create a new one. Once that folder is open press Upload on the toolbar and choose a file, or group of files, on the device to have them added. Alternatively select any OneDrive file or folder and press Download to store it locally.

Previous Versions

One of OneDrive's neatest tricks is to keep old versions of documents in case you need them later. Just single-click any file, press the '...' icon on the toolbar and choose Version History. Older versions will be listed on the left-hand side. Click an old version and you can have it restored or downloaded.

Hot Tip

OneDrive loves photos, and you can bring up a gallery of all the photos stored on your drive by clicking the Photos tab on the left.

Above: OneDrive is available for iPhone.

OneDrive on Other Devices

If you have an iPhone, iPad or Android device you can download a OneDrive app to access files. Just grab it from the relevant app store to access your files from any device.

Edit Documents in OneDrive Online

OneDrive includes a basic version of Word, Excel and PowerPoint, which you can use to make changes and amendments to documents.

1. Click any document in OneDrive to open a preview.

2. Click Edit Document on the toolbar.

3. Choose Edit in Word online.

4. You can now edit and delete text as appropriate.

5. If you're looking for a specific task, like adding comments, you can search for it in the toolbar, or use the Ribbon.

6. When you're done working, click File. From here you can save the file back to OneDrive, locally to your device, share it or even download in a different format such as PDF or ODT (an open-source office document).

Above: OneDrive features web versions of Office.

Above: You can edit and create PowerPoint presentations on the web.

USER ACCOUNTS

Most family PCs have more than one user, but that doesn't mean everyone has to use your login. You can set the whole family up with their own Microsoft IDs, which enables them to personalize their experience and allows you to keep kids safe when they use the PC.

ADDING A NEW ACCOUNT

In Windows 10 there are two types of accounts for secondary users of your device – family and 'other users'. Essentially, when you start adding family members it means when you set up Windows 10 on new devices, their accounts will pop up too, saving the hassle of changing up a whole household of users. That privilege isn't extended to 'other users'.

Set up a Family Member

In your family group, adults are able to manage requests and change settings on the children's account. Anyone added as a family member must use a Microsoft ID.

Above: You can add accounts for everyone in your family.

To set up a family member:

1. Search 'accounts' in Cortana.

2. Choose Family and other users from the left pane and then Add family member.

3. Choose whether you're adding a child or an adult.

4. If any user has a Microsoft ID then use that when prompted.

5. If you want to create an ID for them, tap or click 'The person who I want to add doesn't have an email address' and go through the short sign-up process.

6. Complete the process and they will be added to the list of users.

Above: Children can have their own protected accounts.

Set Up a Non-Family Account

A non-family member can be set up with or without a Microsoft ID. The process is exactly the same as above, but differs if you want to work without an ID.

1. Go to Accounts in the Settings menu and choose Family and other users.

2. Tap or click Add someone else to this PC.

3. If you don't want to use a Microsoft ID, then choose 'I don't have this person's sign-in information'.

4. Now choose 'Add a user without a Microsoft account'.

5. Add a user name.

6. At this point you can progress without entering a password if you wish.

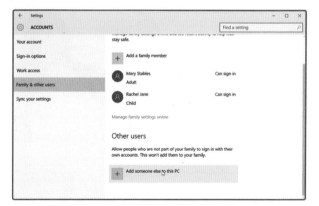

Above: Guests can have accounts outside your family group.

SECURE CHILDREN'S ACCOUNTS

Once you've set up a child's account in Windows 10 there are heaps of tools to keep them safe when using the PC. Here's how to protect young users.

1. On your Windows 10 PC, go to Start > Settings > Accounts > Family & other users.

2. Select Manage family settings online. This will open a web page where you can manage settings.

3. You'll see a list of any children's accounts you've added. Select the child whose settings you want to manage.

Recent Activity

As an adult administrator of the account you can receive a full report of what your children have been up to online. The report allows you to see the websites they visit, apps and games

they've been using, and how much time they've been spending on their devices.

Web Browsing

This option enables you to choose the websites your child can and can't see. Turn on Block appropriate content to add filters to their account. Once this is turned on you can also add undesirable URLs at the bottom to block specific sites.

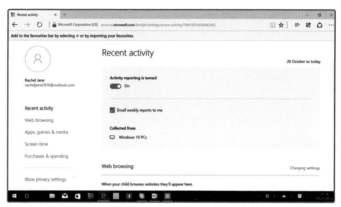

Above: You can get a report of what your child has been up to on the PC.

Apps and Games

Playing games is great for kids, but you can limit the titles your child can download from the Windows Store using age filters. If you want to block specific games you need to do that from the Recent activity tab.

Hot Tip

Kids can't spend money on apps by default, but you can put small amounts of money in their account in the Purchases & spending option.

Screen Time

You can use the parental controls to set time limits for the computer. You can create rules where kids can't use the PC before or after a certain time of day, and choose a maximum amount of screen time for the day.

Above: Child accounts enable you to limit screen time.

NETWORKS

Most people have more than one PC in the home, and it can be frustrating when one PC has a file on its hard drive, but you're using the other machine. That's where networking comes in.

NETWORK YOUR PCS

Networking means linking your PCs together in your home so they act as one giant machine. You can break down the restrictions of which PC your data is stored on, and share things such as external storage and printers. Sound good? Well, the good news is that Windows 10 makes it easy to set up.

WINDOWS HOMEGROUP

A HomeGroup is Windows 10's name for a group of PCs on a home network that can share files and printers. HomeGroup is available in Windows 10, Windows 8 and Windows 7.

What Can a HomeGroup Do?

Using a HomeGroup makes sharing easier. You can share pictures, music, videos, documents and printers with other people and devices in your HomeGroup.

After you create or join a HomeGroup, you select the folders and locations on your Windows 10 PC (for example, My Pictures or My Documents) that you want to share. You can prevent specific files or folders from being shared, and you can share additional libraries later.

Hot Tip

If you're having problems with HomeGroup it might be because network sharing is turned off. You can turn sharing on by going to Settings, choosing Change PC Settings and clicking or tapping the Network option. Choose Connections and then make sure Find devices and content is turned on.

Creating a HomeGroup

When you set up a PC with Windows 10 a HomeGroup is automatically created on the first PC. It's then up to you to add other devices to the group. It will then be enabled automatically unless you opted out of sharing data between PCs when you turned Windows 10 on for the first time. Here's how to set it up:

1. Use Cortana to search for HomeGroup.

Above: HomeGroups let you create networked PCs quickly and easily.

Above: The first PC you set up will create the HomeGroup.

2. Create a HomeGroup.

3. Select the libraries and devices that you want to share with the HomeGroup. You can opt to not share things like movies or videos or pictures, for example, but allow documents.

4. Make a note of the password, as you'll need it for other machines.

Adding Your Other PCs to the HomeGroup

There's no point in setting up a HomeGroup with one PC, so log into your next Windows 7, Windows 8 or Windows 10 PC and join your new group.

1. Find the HomeGroup password on the original PC by going to the items in the Settings. To do that, swipe in from the right edge of the screen, tapping Settings, PC settings, and then tapping or clicking Network followed by HomeGroup. The password will be displayed at the bottom of the screen.

2. Go to the PC you want to join the network and follow the steps above.

3. Enter the HomeGroup password, then tap or click Join.

4. Select the libraries and devices that you want to share with the HomeGroup.

Hot Tip

Any PC that is hibernating or off won't be visible within the HomeGroup and you won't be able to access files. If this is a common problem, you can change the length of time your PC stays awake for in the Power Options menu.

Above: The password can be used for other PCs to join the group.

Finding HomeGroup Files

The other devices in your network will now appear in File Explorer. HomeGroup PCs will appear at the bottom. Click a PC and you can see the shared libraries and view the files inside.

Sharing Libraries

When you create or join a HomeGroup, you select the libraries and devices you want to share with other people. Libraries are initially shared with read access only, but to make sharing truly two way just right-click the folder in File Explorer, click or tap Share with, choose Specific people and then change the permission level from Read to Read/write next to the HomeGroup.

Above: Once in the HomeGroup you can share files.

PRINT WITH YOUR WINDOWS 10 PC

Setting up printers in Windows 10 is a very painless experience, thanks to the incredible breadth of devices supported by Windows 10 out of the box. Just follow these steps to getting yours set up in no time.

SET UP YOUR PRINTER

One of Window 10's greatest strengths is its huge library of devices, which will be recognized as soon as you plug them in. That means that setting up a new printer should be as easy as plug-and-play. This will also work with wireless printers if they're properly connected to the network.

1.   Connect your printer to the PC via the supplied cable.

2.   From the Start menu click Settings > Devices.

3.   In Devices choose Printers
     & scanners.

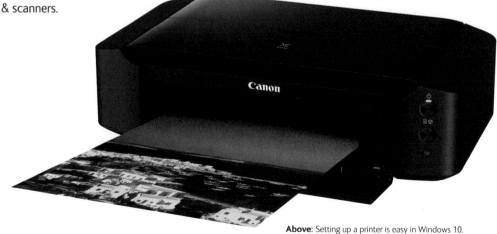

Above: Setting up a printer is easy in Windows 10.

4. From the right pane, under the Add printers & scanners section, click Add a printer or scanner.

5. Wait while Windows searches for the connected printer.

If it Wasn't that Simple...

Of course problems sometimes occur, and what kind of helpful guide would this be if we didn't account for a stubborn printer? If things didn't work out as above, then try the following:

Above: Windows10 supports thousands of printers so yours should plug and play.

1. If Windows cannot detect the connected printer, click the 'The printer that I want isn't listed' link.

2. Click to select Add a local printer or network printer with manual settings.

3. On the Choose a printer port window, leave the default options selected.

4. When you see Install the printer driver, choose from the displayed list of printer manufacturers in the left section, click to select the one to which the connected printer belongs.

Above: If a printer isn't listed grab the drivers from the manufacturer's website.

5. From the right section, locate and click to select the specific model of the printer that is connected to the PC.

6. Input the name and then add its location so other PCs on your network can find it.

HOW TO PRINT IN WINDOWS 10

In most applications you can print a page by choosing File > Print or hitting Ctrl + P. This will bring up the printer dialogue box, which contains all the settings you will need. Just choose the printer you're going to use from the list and then hit Print.

Hot Tip

Again, the PC that your printer is connected to must be on, or other devices won't be able to print.

Print to PDF

You can also 'print to PDF' which is a new feature to Windows 10. Instead of printing the page physically, this feature exports it to a handy PDF file which can be read on most devices.

Above: Just go to File and Print.

Orientation and Page Selection

In the printer dialogue box you can choose whether the page is printed landscape or portrait. You can also choose to have specific pages of your document printed in the Pages drop-down menu. Click More settings to change the paper size.

SHARING A PRINTER

If you have a printer that's connected to a PC using a USB cable, you can share it across your HomeGroup. Networking your printer using a Windows 10 HomeGroup is much simpler than setting up a normal network printer. The downside is that you'll have to have it physically connected to your PC.

1. To share your printer, open HomeGroup by searching using Cortana.

2. Click on Advanced sharing settings and then Turn on file and printer sharing.

3. Open the Print menu of the application you want to print from and hit Ctrl + P, or click or tap File > Print.

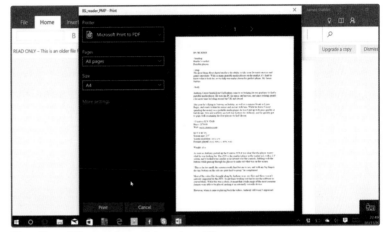

Above: Print to PDF exports documents in easy to read files.

Hot Tip

Change between landscape and portrait orientation under Preferences in the Print dialogue box.

Above: You can share printers between HomeGroup PCs.

MICROSOFT ONENOTE

Whether it's planning a holiday, organizing a school project or just keeping a bunch of recipes, Microsoft OneNote is a fantastic scrapbooking and notetaking app. And it's built right into Windows 10. Here's how to use it.

CREATE A NOTEBOOK IN ONENOTE

When you first open OneNote, it may not be immediately apparent how you get note-taking, but here's how to dive in and start organizing.

Getting Started

The basis of OneNote is Notebooks. You can have as many as you like but keep one Notebook for each topic, for example, recipes, next January's trip to Iceland, redecorating ideas and so on. Each Notebook can have multiple sub-sections, which in turn can have multiple pages. Just tap + Page to add a new one to the left-hand pane and tap or click to select it. Right-click to rename a page.

Above: OneNote is a great scrapbooking app.

What Can You Add?

You can add pretty much anything you like to a page. Copy text from web pages, cut and paste images, maps, type or even hand write notes – it's all fair game. From most Windows apps just hit the Share button and then choose OneNote to have the information added.

OneNote's interface can be a little confusing, but here's how to get started:

1. Add a title for your page.

2. Add a page to the section.

3. Click to add sections to the Notebook and right-click to rename.

4. The main menu for managing your Notebooks.

Above: You can share web content with OneNote to import easily.

5. Access highlighter and hand drawing tools.

6. Add boxes to your pages for questions, contacts, addresses etc.

CALENDAR

The Calendar app in Windows 10 is an extremely efficient way of getting organized. Just by opening the Calendar app you've acquired a powerful cloud-based diary that's available across devices. So ditch the pen and paper diary and try this universal app instead.

WORK WITH OLD CALENDARS OR START AFRESH

If you've previously used Hotmail or Outlook calendars you'll see them as soon as you load the Windows 10 app. If not, it's a clean slate to work on. The beauty of the Windows 10 Calendar is that it syncs with your Microsoft ID, which means any additions can be seen across any device you log into.

Import Your Existing Calendar

The likelihood is that you'll already have an online calendar in a different app. That's fine because the Calendar in Windows 10 can import and sync with virtually any service.

Above: The Calendar is a powerful tool in Windows 10.

1. Click the 'hamburger' icon – the three lines in the top left that summon the left pane.

2. Click or tap the Settings icon, represented by a cog.

3. Choose Accounts in the right menu.

4. Hit Add account.

5. Choose the service from the list.

6. Enter your credentials for the account that your calendar currently uses.

Quickly Add Events
To add an event to your calendar just click or tap a day. A new box will open and you can write the name and time. Hit enter and it will be added.

Add Detailed Events
Calendar events are more than just about times and dates. By clicking the + New event button in the left pane you can create events which recur every day, week, month or year; add locations and even invite your contacts to attend.

Above: You can bring in multiple accounts into the Calendar app.

Create New Calendars
You can also have multiple calendars, so you can separate your work and personal life. To create these you'll need to log into http://calendar.live.com. Click the cog in the top right and choose Options > Add new calendar. This will now appear in the Windows 10 app.

Above: Just click a square to add an event.

Toggle Calendars
Once you have multiple calendars in Windows 10 you can toggle them on and off within the app. Just open the left pane and tick or untick the calendars as required.

Personalize
You can give your Windows 10 Calendar app a personal look by clicking or tapping the cog icon in the left pane. Choose Personalization and then select the colours, themes and backgrounds to suit your taste.

LOOK, WATCH AND PLAY

PHOTOS

The Photos app is the universal way to view, edit and show off your pictures and memories across Windows 10 devices. It's a one stop shop for all the pictures on your PC and OneDrive too.

ACCESS YOUR PHOTOS

The Photos app in Windows 10 is the perfect way to view your photos. The old Windows Photo Viewer still exists in the desktop element of Windows 10, but it pales in comparison when it comes to the amount of options and usability on touch-screen displays. Just search 'photos' in Cortana or choose Photos from the apps list.

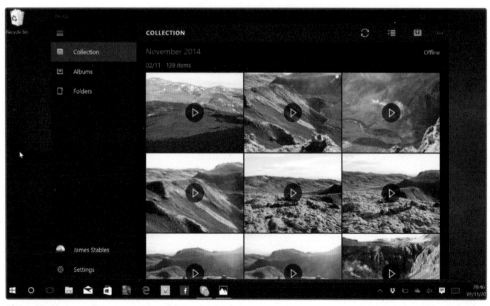

Above: The Photos app lets you view, edit and share your snaps.

Collections

When you open the Photos app, the first thing you will see is the Collections window. This orders your photos by the date taken and groups them together. You can then scroll down through all the photos, tapping one to make it full screen.

Albums

When you access the Albums screen for the first time you'll see your pictures grouped by date, much like the Collections. However, unlike Collections, an album is designed to be a handpicked selection of your best shots. You can create a new album by choosing the + icon in the top right, or by tapping or clicking any of the suggested albums.

Customize Your Albums

In the resulting screen you can change the placeholder information using the pen icon at the top. You can give your album a name and also choose a cover photo by tapping or clicking Change cover. This brings up a new window, which lets you choose a

Above: The Photos app sorts your photos into collections.

Hot Tip

Just tap or click the date within the Collections screen to get a list of dates, which makes it easier to get to the photos you want.

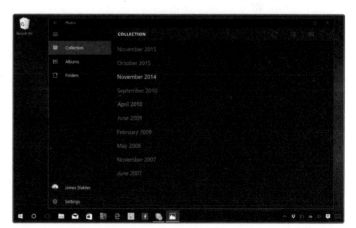

Above: By default photos are sorted by month taken.

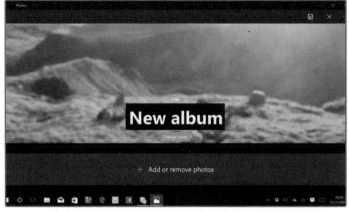

Above: You can create your own albums of any of your photos.

Hot Tip

Create a completely custom album by tapping the +
icon at the top and selecting photos for the album.

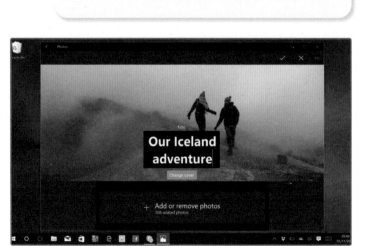

Above: You can choose a name for your album and the cover shot.

photo to represent your album.
You can then click the Add or
remove photos option, which lets
you select or deselect photos to
be included in the album.

Folders

The Folders screen shows all of
the locations on your Windows
10 PC where the Photos app will
drag in pictures. By default it will
look for snaps in your pictures
library, the same library in
OneDrive and the public folder.
However, you can add new
folders if your pictures are stored
elsewhere.

1. Click the settings cog
   in the bottom of the
   left-hand column.

2. Under sources tap
   Add a folder.

3. Find the folder in the
   new window.

4. Choose Add this folder
   to Pictures.

Hot Tip

You can choose any shot to be the Live Tile for the Photos app by heading to the Settings menu and changing the option to 'a single photo'. Just select the shot you'd like from the new window that appears.

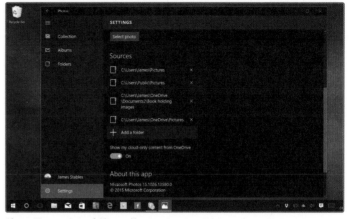

Above: You can set any folder as a library.

Slideshow

You can start a slideshow of any of your photos at any time. Just go to any collection or album and choose the first photo in the list. The slideshow button is located in the toolbar at the top. Alternatively you can hit the F5 button on your keyboard.

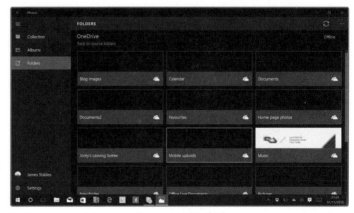

Above: The Photos app will show photos stored in OneDrive.

EDIT YOUR PHOTOS

If your editing needs are more advanced than a simple crop, then the Photos app is here to help you. When you're viewing a photo, just tap or click the edit icon in the top menu. New options will appear on the left and right of the screen.

Above: There is a host of editing options in the photo app.

Hot Tip

By default all pictures viewed in the Photos app are auto-enhanced. See the difference by toggling the enhancements on and off by tapping or clicking the option in the top menu bar.

Basic Fixes

Your photos can be improved hugely with relatively simple edits. Just hit the basic fixes option on the left and a new menu of fixes will appear on the right. These include:

- **Rotate**: Turn a sideways photo clockwise. Just keep tapping to keep turning until it's the right way up.

- **Crop**: Trim a photo and focus in on the best bits. Just drag the box to change what's included.

- **Straighten**: Pictures look better with a straight horizon. Tap and hold the Straighten icon and then turn the dial in either direction.

- **Red eye**: If any devil eyes appear in your shots just choose the icon and then tap or click on the offending peepers.

- **Retouch**: Remove blemishes, spots and other unwanted items just by tapping or clicking Retouch and then clicking any offending spot.

Filters

Apps like Instagram have brought filters into vogue, and you can add your own to any shot in the Photos app. Just tap the Filters option on the left and then select an effect from the right. You get six different filters to choose from – just click to apply.

Above: Add Instagram-style filters to your snaps for a retro look.

Light

This option lets you control the brightness, contrast, highlights and shadows within your photos. To apply the changes, just click and hold your mouse on the option, or tap with your finger on touch-screen devices. Then just drag outwards to increase or decrease the light in the photo. The changes will be previewed on screen.

Colour

This option enables you to change the temperature (how warm the colours are), add tints, change the saturation of the colours and enhance the colours in your photos. The first three options require you to press and hold to change the levels, while Colour Boost requires you to select the option, tap or click on the area you want to enhance and then use the white arrow to change the levels in that area.

Effects

The last two effects are two of the best in the Photo app: the ability to add a vignette and add a focus point to your

Hot Tip

When an effect is applied it's not permanent until you save it. If you've gone too far with your edits, you can press the back button on the top bar or hit the X to discard the changes.

Above: The selective focus tool lets you blur out parts of your shot.

images. A vignette is a vintage-style darkening of the corners, which you can control after holding your mouse or finger on the option.

The selective focus option puts a box on the screen, which you can drag to place and resize. Everything outside that circle will be blurred, while everything inside will stay crisp.

AFTER EDITING

Once you've got your shots how you like them, it's time to save and share them with friends and family. Windows 10 puts sharing front and centre, offering a near seamless experience between your favourite apps.

Compare to the Original

When you're busy making edits it can become a little confusing whether you've improved things or gone over the top. Click the Compare to original button on the top bar to quickly flick back to the unedited shot.

Save

Once you're happy, you can save over the original by choosing the Save button from the top. This will replace the original, whichever folder it's stored in.

Save a Copy

If you've got a bit creative and you don't want to save over the original, that's fine. Just choose the Save a copy button at the top to create a new file in the original location.

Share

The best thing about photos and memories is sharing them with loved ones. In Windows 10 you can do this straight from the Photos app. Just come out of editing mode and then click the Share icon on the top bar. A new menu will appear from the right, and you can choose to share via email or through apps like Facebook and Twitter. Just tap the app you want to use to get started.

Do More

When viewing any photo in the app, just click on the three little dots in the top right-hand corner of the screen. You then get options to open the file in a different Windows 10 app, which could be other photo editors you've downloaded from the Windows Store. You can also print the photo from this menu.

Above: You can quickly share photos on social networks with the Photos app.

MUSIC

The Groove Music app in Windows 10 replaces the now defunct Xbox Music service from Windows 8. However, it does much the same thing. You can use it to play all of the music held on your PC, or pay for a monthly pass to stream unlimited music from a library of over 30 million songs. Sound good? Read on for the basics.

Above: Groove Music replaced Xbox Music in Windows 10.

FIND AND PLAY MUSIC

Most people have bulging collections of music held on their PC in MP3 format, and Groove Music is the best place in Windows 10 to play it. To open Groove just search for it using Cortana, or you can find it in the apps list on the Start menu.

Find Your Music

Groove Music is set by default to find music held in your PC's Music library, whether stored locally on your PC or on OneDrive.

Add More Locations

If you want to add music that's held outside of these locations, then click the settings cog at the bottom of the left-hand pane. Click Choose where we look for music and then find the folder in the resulting menu.

Above: Groove Music will look in your Music library for songs by default.

The Groove Music app is simply laid out and easy to use.

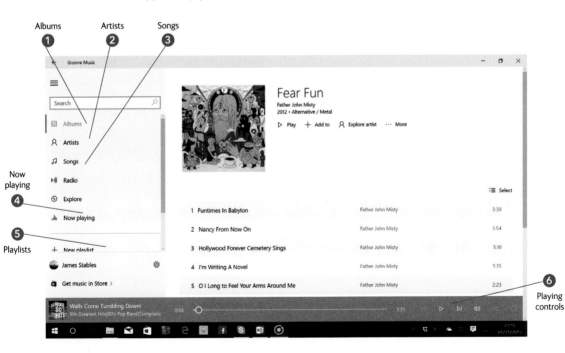

Albums 1 Artists 2 Songs 3

Now playing 4

Playlists 5

Playing controls 6

1 **Albums**

Get a list of all the albums on your PC.

2 **Artists**

Browse all artists in alphabetical order.

3 **Songs**

A complete list of all songs.

4 **Now playing**

The order of tracks being played currently.

5 **Playlists**

You can create a new playlist from here, which will then be added below.

6 **Playing controls**

You can start, stop and change the volume of playback in this part of the screen.

Hot Tip

iTunes users can automatically import their tracks to Groove Music. Click the cog menu and choose Import iTunes playlists.

Above: Playlists are collections of songs you can edit together.

Create a Playlist

You can group tracks together in playlists, creating workout playlists or party ones quickly and easily. Just choose the New Playlist button in the left-hand column and then Give it a name. Then browse your music, right-clicking on any song and adding it to that playlist. You can also drag and drop songs to add.

Pin Music to Start Menu

If you have an album of artists you just can't stop listening to, then you can pin it to the Start menu so you can get listening faster. Just click any playlist, album or artist and then choose the More button. Tap or click Pin to Start to have it linked.

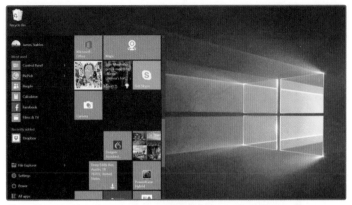

Above: You can add an album, song or artists to your Start menu for quick access.

LISTEN TO WINDOWS 10 MUSIC ANYWHERE

OneDrive lets you access your files anywhere, and it does the same with your music. Groove isn't just available for your PC – you can download it for your Windows 10 phone (it's a universal app, after all) and for iOS and Android handsets as well. Gone are the days Windows users were locked out of other types of devices.

Add Music

The Groove Music app will find any MP3 files in your OneDrive music library and play them

Hot Tip

To start your own 'radio station' of similar music to a particular artist or song you like, just right-click any Groove Music item and choose Start radio. You will need a Groove Music Pass.

Above: Groove Music will play songs stored on your OneDrive across any device.

Above: Groove is also available as an iOS app.

within the smartphone app. You can do this in File Explorer. Just move any music you want to play from the app into the Music folder located in OneDrive.

Download Apps

As well as being a universal app for Windows 10 devices, the Groove app is available for both iOS and Android. Just grab it from the respective store to get started.

Sign In With a Windows ID

Once downloaded you just need to sign in with your Microsoft ID. This will trawl your OneDrive libraries for music files and import them. It will also source any playlists you've made in Groove Music.

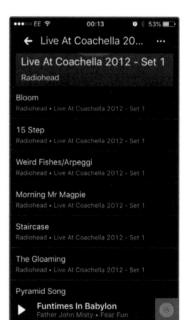

Above: Add music to your PC's OneDrive folder and it will appear on your phone.

Start Listening

You can then start browsing for music just as you would on your PC. Tap the icon with three lines in the top left to bring up the sidebar menu, from which you can navigate to specific playlists or your entire collection. If you're using a Groove Music Pass you can access the service's built-in radio.

Save for Offline Access

Groove will stream tracks from your OneDrive library, which will require your phone to have a data connection or otherwise be connected to a Wi-Fi network. However, you can avoid unwanted billing surprises by saving tracks and playlists offline. Just long press on any album, playlist or track and choose Make available offline to have it downloaded to your device.

Turn Off Mobile Data

If you're worried about Groove Music eating into your monthly allowance you can opt to switch off its access to data. In the left-hand menu just go to Settings and then switch off Use mobile data. The Groove app will now wait until you have a Wi-Fi connection before downloading or streaming music.

TRY THE GROOVE MUSIC STORE

Groove Music puts over 30 million songs at your fingertips with the Groove Music Pass. You can get a free 30-day trial to see what it's all about. The full price after the trial is £8.99/$9.99 per month.

Start the Trial

To start the free trial just head to the Groove app in Windows 10. It can be accessed by searching with Cortana or looking in the apps list on the Start menu. Once in the app choose to browse music from the Store in the left-hand column, and the app will snap to the left, while the Windows Store opens to the right. There will be a link to start the Groove Music Pass trial.

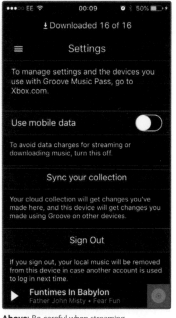

Above: Be careful when streaming music as it can be costly.

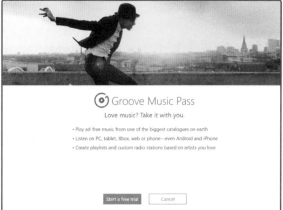

Above: You get a one month free trial of Groove's streaming service.

Add Your Banking Information

Click or tap to start the trial and you'll be prompted to enter your Windows 10 Hello PIN number to confirm your identity. You will then need to enter your billing information.

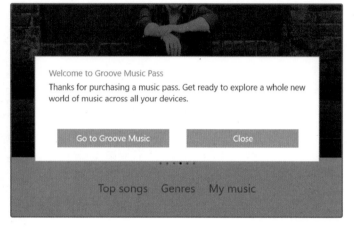

Above: You'll need to access your bank information to start the trial.

Search for Songs

Once you've signed up for the Groove Music Pass it's time to find some tunes. Using the search bar in the left you can find any album, artist or song that takes your fancy. The results will appear in the middle window, and you just double-click or tap to play.

Build a Library of Songs

Once you start finding music you like, you can start building up a personal collection. On any album or track you can press the + to add it to your collection or have it placed into a playlist.

Above: Don't forget to cancel the trial if you don't want to get charged.

Get Out of the Trial Before You Pay

You get 30 days free, but as soon as that period is up you will be billed. If you don't fancy continuing with Groove Music Pass and its 30 million songs, then you can leave by clicking the cog icon and then clicking or tapping Manage Subscription. A new Edge browser window will open and your Microsoft account information will appear. You can see when you'll be charged and can cancel the trial accordingly.

WINDOWS MEDIA PLAYER

The Groove app does have its limitations for hardcore music fans, and it doesn't play back higher-quality music files. That's where Windows Media Player comes in. It's been a staple of Windows for years, and hasn't really changed since Windows 7. But in many ways, if you're not interested in using a Groove Music Pass in Windows 10, it's a good way to listen to your music.

Above: Windows Media Player is still going strong in Windows 10.

Open Windows Media Player

To open Windows Media Player, search for it in Cortana. It's not pinned to the taskbar by default, so now is a good opportunity to keep it there for easy access next time. While it's open and on the taskbar, right-click and choose Pin to Taskbar.

Find Your Media in Windows Media Player

When you start Windows Media Player for the first time it will scan your libraries for all media files. You can find them through the music, video and pictures options in the left-hand pane; just click or tap the option to display your music in the main window and double-click a song or video to play it.

If you need to add video or music that's not in your libraries, it's easy. Go to any File Explorer folder and click the Organize tab on the taskbar, click Manage libraries and then choose music or video. A new box will open which shows the folders that Windows Media Player classifies as libraries. Press add and navigate to any folder and choose Include folder.

Hot Tip

When playing music, Windows Media Player will accompany the sound with visualizations, which are moving images that go along with the tune. You can browse for more by going to Organize > Options and clicking the Plug-ins tab. Click Look for visualizations on the web.

Above: Again, you can add any folder to Media Player's library.

RIP CDS TO YOUR PC

One of the best features of Windows Media Player is its ability to turn your CDs into digital music files and store them on your PC. This process is known as 'ripping' and it's perfectly legal as long as you own the CD in the first place.

Hot Tip

If you want to change the order of the items in the burn list, drag them up or down the list.

Ripping CDs means you can have your entire music collection on your PC, so it can be played and enjoyed in more ways, not to mention backed up. So even if your original CDs are destroyed, stolen or get scratched you still have your music.

When you rip music from a CD, you're copying songs from an audio CD to your PC. During the ripping process, the Player compresses each song and stores it on your drive as a Windows Media Audio (WMA), WAV, or MP3 file.

Above: You can copy CDs to your PC using Media Player, if you have a CD drive.

1. Make sure your PC is connected to the Internet if you want Windows Media Player to automatically get info about the songs, such as the name of the CD, the artist and titles for the tracks.

2. Open Windows Media Player.

3. Insert an audio CD into the PC's CD drive.

4. Tap or click the Rip CD button.

Above: You can also burn songs to a CD.

TV AND VIDEO

Windows 10 has multiple ways to watch films, TV shows and any video on your PC, making it an excellent hub for all your entertainment. So kick back, relax and let us show you how to get started.

Above: Films & TV is the default movie player in Windows 10.

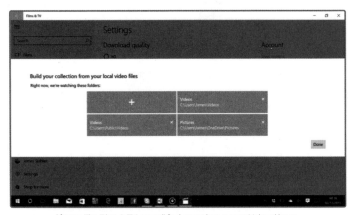

Above: The Films & TV app will find any videos in your Videos library.

PLAYING YOUR VIDEOS IN THE FILMS & TV APP

The Films & TV app in Windows 10 is a direct upgrade from the Xbox Movies one in Windows 8. You can buy, rent and watch films or TV shows here, as well as view videos you've filmed yourself.

Import Videos

The Windows 10 Films & TV app will automatically detect any video files in the Videos library, either in Windows 10 or OneDrive. However, you can add extra locations quickly and easily. That's particularly handy if you have movie clips or videos shot on your phone or digital camera in your Pictures library.

Above: You can watch videos full screen on your device.

To add extra locations just go to the Settings menu in the left-hand column and tap or click Choose where we look for videos. Click the + and navigate to the desired folder and press OK. You can repeat the process until you have all your videos imported. You'll find them in the Videos tab.

Watch Videos

You will now see thumbnails and titles for all your stored videos. To watch one just double-click or tap the preview to start playing. When the video launches you will see a host of on-screen controls, where you can pause, fast-forward or rewind.

Buy and Rent Videos

The Windows Store isn't just for apps and games – you can buy and rent films and TV shows too. Just head to the Film or TV tab and you'll see a small selection. Click or tap Choose more to be whisked off to the Windows Store. Tap or click a film you fancy and you will have the option to buy or rent it at different prices.

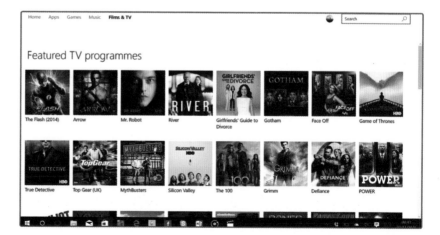

Right: You can buy and rent movies through the app.

Above: Rentals expire after 14 days.

Renting Movies

When you rent a film you can choose whether to stream it or download it to your device. When you download a movie it will stay for 14 days, but when you press play you will have 24 hours to finish it before it disappears from your PC.

Play to Other Devices

If you're playing a video, movie or TV show from your Windows 10 PC in the Films & TV app, you can have it cast to another device, such as a console or TV. This means you can sit back and enjoy your content on the big screen without hooking up any cables or laborious data transfers. Just play the video and then choose Cast to next to the play button. Available devices on your network will appear – just click to cast.

Hot Tip

In the Films & TV app you can change between colour and black and white. Just click the Settings cog and then change the theme.

WATCH A DVD IN WINDOWS 8.1

The Films & TV app is great for renting and buying content, but if you want to watch a DVD you're out of luck. However, there are a couple of options you can use instead.

Try VLC Player

The best option is to download the free VLC Player from http://www.videolan.org. This powerful player can handle any kind of video file, and comes highly recommended. Just download the app and insert a DVD into your optical drive. Open VLC and you will see your DVD in the left-hand pane. You can also download a version from the Windows Store.

Above: You don't have to watch Hollywood blockbusters.

Or Use Windows Media Player

The built-in Windows Media Player can also handle DVDs. Just pop your DVD in the drive and it should be automatically recognized by Media Player. You can also open it up by double clicking it in the left-hand pane and choosing a title menu to play.

Above: VLC Player is a powerful video player available from the Windows Store.

GAMING IN WINDOWS 10

PCs and gaming have always gone hand in hand, and Windows 10 offers even more ways to take a break from the stresses of everyday life and enjoy some seriously immersive experiences. From quick games from the Windows Store to the latest blockbusters and Xbox classics, Windows 10 is seriously strong for gaming.

PLAYING GAMES FROM THE WINDOWS STORE

The Windows Store is a great place to download games for your Windows 10 PC. What's more, many are universal apps, which means you can put down the game on one device and pick up the action on another.

Above: Gaming is a huge part of Windows 10.

Finding Games in the Windows Store

The Windows Store has a dedicated area for downloading games. Just head to the store via the icon on the taskbar or search in Cortana. When the app loads just head to the Games tab to start browsing.

Playing Games You Install

When you install any game from the Windows Store it will be added in a number of places. Firstly, you'll find it in the Start menu under All Apps; new installations will be added to the top. You will also find it in the Xbox app – but more on that later.

Hot Tip
Games tend to open within a window that you can maximize from the title bar, which will remain visible. You can go full screen by clicking the arrow icon. Hover your mouse at the top to bring it back to close the game when you're ready.

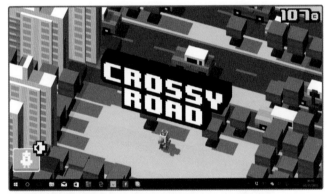

Above: There are hundreds of free games to play from Windows Store.

Above: In Windows 10, Xbox controllers just plug and play using a standard USB cable.

Connect an Xbox Controller

All games from the Windows Store work with your PC's keyboard, but you can hook up an Xbox controller to your PC to really amp up the fun. The latest wireless Xbox One controllers have a standard USB plug in the top. Just hook it into your PC and you're ready to go – no installation required.

Try Steam

The Windows Store has plenty of fun games to keep you interested, but most are ported versions of mobile apps. If you want to try your hand at serious gaming, try Steam. It's a huge marketplace of the greatest titles of all time – which you can download onto your PC to play. Try it at http://store.steampowered.com

XBOX APP IN WINDOWS 10

Microsoft isn't just the maker of Windows 10, it's also behind the hugely successful Xbox One, one of the most popular consoles available. In Windows 10 the company has brought the two together through the Xbox app, which lets you not only manage your account, but also play games with Xbox users and even stream games to your PC.

Accessing the Xbox App

To fire up the app just ask Cortana for 'Xbox' or look for the app in the All Apps menu in Start.

Above: The Xbox app is a second screen to your console.

If you have an Xbox everything should be pretty familiar, and your Gamertag and avatar will be present. If you've never played Xbox before, that's no problem. You can start all that stuff from here, no purchase required.

The Xbox App Explained

The Xbox app is extremely busy when it first loads with many menus to explore. You'll enter on the home screen where you'll get a breakdown of your recently played games and what your friends (if you've made any on Xbox Live) are up to. Then you'll see the following menus down the side.

○ **Profile**: Your avatar, profile options and list of activity, achievements, game captures and more.

○ **Home**: All your friends' activity information.

○ **My Games**: A list of all your titles.

○ **Messages**: Where you send and receive messages from other gamers.

○ **Alerts**: Notifications on messages and invites.

○ **Achievements**: In-game awards for completing missions.

○ **Game DVR**: Your saved in-game clips ready for viewing and editing.

○ **Windows Store**: Download or buy new games for your Windows 10 PC.

○ **OneGuide**: TV listings via a connected Xbox One.

○ **Connect**: This is where you can hook up your Xbox One if it's on the same network.

○ **Settings**: Tweak elements of the Xbox app.

Using the Xbox App Without an Xbox

As we mentioned, there's absolutely no need for you to own an Xbox in order to take advantage of the app in Windows 10. You can use it as a hub for your existing downloaded games from the Windows Store. Just got to the My Games in the left-hand column and tap or click play to launch any game.

Buying Games From the Store

You can click the Windows Store icon to go and download games. When they finish downloading, they will appear in the Xbox app, ready to play.

Chat With Friends

You can send in-game messages to friends with the Xbox app, whether you're playing on your Windows 10 PC or your console. It's virtually impossible to send coherent messages with your control pad, which makes the Windows 10 app a fantastic companion device. Just go to the

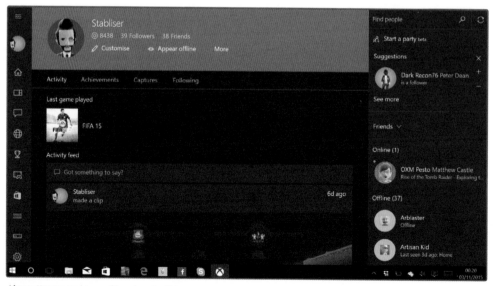

Above: You can see your profile and gaming history.

Messages tab in the left column, click + New Message and then choose an Xbox friend.

PC Versus Xbox Gaming

Some games enable you to play against Xbox players from the comfort of your PC, which is fairly mind-bendingly futuristic. The biggest title is Fable Legends but you can also play against Xbox owners with Gigantic, Game 4 and Siegecraft Commander.

Above: Games like Fable Legends can be played against Xbox users.

Advanced Settings

You can make tweaks to the way the Xbox app works by clicking the cog icon at the bottom of the left-hand toolbar. The most interesting options here are to sign in with a different Xbox Live account, should you be using different Microsoft IDs for whatever reason. There are also options to up the quality, which we'll come on to in the next section.

Hot Tip

Using an Ethernet connection (or Powerline connection, if your PC is too far from your router) should keep things nice and speedy if you're suffering lagging or stuttering over Wi-Fi.

STREAM XBOX ONE GAMES TO A WINDOWS 10 PC

One of the niftiest features of the Windows 10 Xbox app is the ability to stream a game from the console and play it on your PC. This is perfect if your living room TV has been taken over but you still fancy shooting some bad guys. Here's how to make it happen.

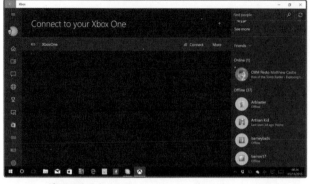

Above: Xbox Connect lets you play your console from your PC.

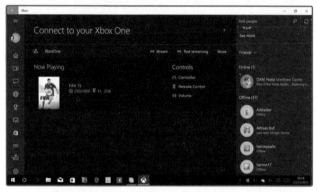

Above: Just make sure your Xbox and PC are on the same network.

Above: Hook up your controller and you're ready to connect.

1. Plug in and set up an Xbox One controller on your Windows 10 PC or tablet. It will be recognized automatically, and will connect using a standard USB lead. At this point turn on your Xbox console and make sure you're signed in.

2. Launch the Xbox app for Windows 10. We're going to assume your account is already linked. Head to the Connect icon in the left-hand pane. Press the plus icon in the top right-hand corner.

3. The Add a device screen will appear. You should see your Xbox listed in the screen. If it's not, then check both devices are turned on and that they are connected to your network. Press the Connect button.

4. A connection to your Xbox will be made and you should be able to see your latest games. At this point you should test the streaming connection, which will help Windows 10 optimize the settings for the best experience. This can take a few minutes.

5. When that's done you're ready to stream. Just hit the Stream button and your screen will become a mirror of your Xbox's. You can now navigate using the Xbox controller and start playing.

Up the Quality

By default you might not think the quality of your stream is very good. However, you can improve it to Xbox-quality graphics in the Settings menu. Just click or tap the cog within the Xbox app for Windows 10 and then click the Xbox One tab. Choose Very high and return to the stream for eye-popping visuals.

RECORD YOUR GAMES

Gaming is becoming increasingly social and recording your gaming sessions is one part of that. This can be for your own pleasure, for uploading to YouTube to show off, or demonstrate to friends how to complete tough parts.

Above: Streaming games means you don't have to hog the TV to have some fun.

Above: You navigate your Xbox just as you would normally, just via your PC.

Above: Head to the Settings menu and max out the quality.

Start Recording

When you're playing a game you can summon the Game bar at any time by pressing the Windows key + G. A new window will appear. There's a big red button here that you can press to start recording everything that happens on screen.

Above: The Game bar can be summoned using the Windows key + G.

Above: The Game bar lets you record your sessions.

Find Your Recordings

One you've recorded a clip, it will be saved in your Videos library in a folder called Captures. It's best accessed via the Xbox app; go to the Game DVR tab and you'll see a list of all your captures.

Edit Your Captures

Your captures will often be a bit too long, probably have a healthy amount of menu browsing, and a fair share of dullness before the real action starts. Luckily, in the Xbox app there's a handful of editing tools to enhance your clips. You can cut boring intros and endings by tapping or clicking Trim and then dragging the sliders inwards. Anything not covered by the blue line will be cut. Click Trim original to cut the file and Save copy to keep the original intact and make a second, edited file.

The Best of Xbox

If you're already an accomplished Xbox user, you'll find your existing game clips in the app. You can find these in the Game DVR menu under the Shared tab. You can play back and edit them on your Windows PC, just like the ones recorded straight from the Game bar.

Hot Tip

You can record using the Game bar even in normal Windows 10 apps. Just open it using the Windows key + G shortcut and press record.

Share

Once you've edited your clip you can share it. In the Xbox app just click Share to post it to your activity feed or direct message it to a friend. Alternatively, from the Videos library you can right-click on the file to put it on Twitter, Facebook or any other social media app.

Above: Game bar captures are stored in the Xbox app.

MAINTAIN

BACKING UP

Your Windows 10 PC is home to so many important and irreplaceable files: photos, memories, projects, coursework and personal documents. But all technology is susceptible to failure and backing up is the key to keeping your data safe.

FILE HISTORY

File History is the main way to back up your PC in Windows 10. Rather than grabbing huge swathes of your files, which can needlessly run into many gigabytes, File History aims to save just your precious files.

What Does File History Back Up?

Essentially, File History finds all the files and folders in your Windows 10 libraries and backs them up constantly (as long as your drive is connected). That means your documents, pictures, videos and music libraries will be protected and, what's more, you can roll back to previous versions of your documents.

Above: File History is the best way to back up.

However, if you have folders outside of these libraries you want backed up, File History can be a little awkward. Turn to pages 167–69 to find out how to handle your libraries.

What Do You Need to Make a Backup?

To back up your files you'll need storage that isn't part of your existing PC's hard drive. While you may see two hard drives (usually

C: and D: drives), these are generally two partitions of the same drive. The options are:

- **An external USB hard drive**: This will need to be at least 16GB in size to use Windows File History.

- **Cloud storage**: OneDrive only offers drag-and-drop syncing, which isn't really a backup. You can buy cloud storage back-up options.

Hot Tip
You can extend the backup to your HomeGroup PCs, so all important files from across your network will be saved in one location.

- **Network attached storage (NAS)**: A hard drive that connects to your router rather than directly to a PC, meaning you can back up all your PCs.

How Much Storage Do You Need?

That totally depends on how many pictures, documents, MP3s and other files you have on your PC. However, 16GB really is the least you need.

How to Start a File History Backup

1. Select the Start button, then select Settings > Update & security > Backup.

2. Plug in your USB hard drive.

3. Click Add a drive and choose the destination drive from the list.

4. Select the libraries you want to be backed up, or deselect the ones you don't.

Above: A USB hard drive is an easy way to back up your files.

Above: Automatic backup will take the hassle out of backing up.

Above: You can manually add folders not covered automatically.

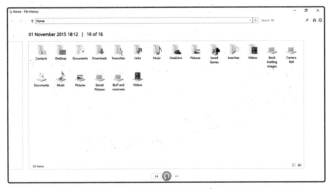

Above: You can then choose to bring specific files and folders back from the dead.

Restore Your Files

If your entire system is wiped, you can restore your files from your external hard drive – that's a given. Just open up the drive and retrieve all your files. However, File History can help you get that file you saved over or accidentally deleted.

If you're missing an important file or folder, here's how to get it back:

1. Search for Restore files from the taskbar and select Restore your files with File History.

2. Look for the file you need and then use the arrows to see all its versions.

3. When you find the version you want, select the Restore button to save it in its original location. To save it in a different place, right-click (or press and hold) the Restore button, select Restore to, and then choose a new location.

BACKUP AND RESTORE (WINDOWS 7)

There is another option for backing up in Windows 10. The old backup and restore feature from Windows 7 has been returned after losing its place in Windows 8.1. It's a more versatile backup option for those whose files live outside their libraries, and you can back up your entire PC if you wish. It doesn't feature the smart file versions of File History.

1. Use Cortana to find 'backup and restore' and select from the list.

2. Attach your storage and select from the list.

3. Tap or click Let me choose.

4. Specify the folders you wish to back up.

5. If you ever need to restore your backup, go to Backup and Restore. If your storage is attached, your backup should be shown.

Above: Backup and Restore remains from Windows 7 and is still a powerful option.

Hot Tip

Backup and Restore isn't as smart as File History, so it will need to run a complete backup as often as possible. You can schedule your backups to run at night when you're not using your PC.

Above: You can back up your entire PC using this tool.

SYSTEM RESTORE

When things go wrong you'll have your backups, but getting your PC back as you had it is a different story. That's where System Restore comes in.

Above: A restore point is a snapshot in time of your PC.

Hot Tip

To use a System Restore point you will need to have System Protection turned on. Do that by going to the System Properties menu. It's awkwardly buried so use Cortana to find it. The go to the System Protection tab and click a drive. Press Configure and then turn it on.

USE SYSTEM IMAGE BACKUP

The System Image feature enables you to take a snapshot of your entire system and save it to an external drive. If the worst were to happen, you could resurrect this image on a new system and have everything back the way it was before.

Going to the File History screen is the best way to create a System Image backup. It's best set up once your PC is working perfectly, and in the event of a disaster, used to recreate your system and then reload your files separately from the File History backup. See opposite for how to restore your PC using a System Image.

1. Choose the System Image Backup option in the bottom left of the File History window.

2. Now choose Create a System Image and the utility will open.

3. Pick a place to save your system image backup (on a hard disk, on one or more DVDs, or on a network location), and click Next.

4. Confirm the settings and choose Start backup.

RESTORE YOUR PC

While you use your PC, Windows 10 automatically takes snapshots of your system to use as a Restore Point – this feature is on by default. If you suffer a PC crash and you need to use System Restore, it's easy.

1. Right-click (or press and hold) the Start button, then select Control Panel.

2. Search Control Panel for Recovery.

3. Select Recovery > Open System Restore > Next.

4. Choose the Restore Point related to the problematic app, driver or update, then select Next > Finish.

Hot Tip

It's advisable to create a System Image in partnership with a File History, rather than instead of. While System Image might seem more comprehensive, it can't keep up the pace of creating a new image every time your files change.

Create a system image

Where do you want to save the backup?

A system image is a copy of the drives required for Windows to run. It can also include additional drives. A system image can be used to restore your computer if your hard drive or computer ever stops working; however, you can't select individual items to restore.

◉ On a hard disk
FreeAgent GoFlex Drive (F:) 1.29 TB free

○ On one or more DVDs

○ On a network location
Select...

Next   Cancel

Above: You'll need plenty of free storage to take a System Image.

DISK CLEAN-UP

The Disk Clean-up feature has been buried in Windows 10, but it's a great tool for quickly decluttering your operating system, which has the dual benefit of making your PC run faster while saving precious hard drive space.

USING DISK CLEAN-UP TO DELETE SYSTEM FILES

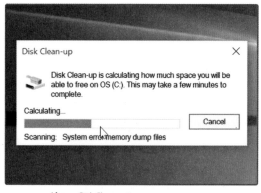

Above: Disk Clean-up is an easy way to reclaim space on your hard drive.

1. To open Disk Clean-up from the desktop, search Administrative Tools, and then double-tap or double-click Disk Clean-up from the next list. In the Drives list, tap or click the drive that you want to clean up, then tap or click OK.

2. You'll now see a host of checkboxes for the types of clutter that can be deleted. Tick as many as you want to delete. A running total of the amount of data you can save will be displayed underneath the list. Press OK when you're done to have those files created.

3. If you really want to start saving space, you can opt to clean up System Files. This will include a host of Windows background information, which while not unnecessary clutter, are not essential for Windows 10's day-to-day running.

Hot Tip

System files that eat up disk space can range from Windows Update log files to User File History.

Above: Tick the boxes you want to have cleaned up.

Above: If you upgraded from Windows 7/8 then look for the mammoth folder of old files, 'Windows.old' – this can be deleted.

TRY CCLEANER

While the basic Windows 10 Disk Clean-up app is great for ridding your system of files, your PC's registry also needs regular cleaning and there's no tool within Windows. A great tool is the free CCleaner, which has a host of options to get your PC back to its best. You can download it from piriform.com/ccleaner

Above: CCleaner is a good, free third party utility.

Hot Tip

If you've upgraded to Windows 10, there will be a huge folder on your PC containing the system files from the previous version of Windows. Find this folder by going to This PC > C: > and looking for the old Windows folder. This can be 20GB in size. You're free to delete it, but make sure all your old photos and documents have been copied over first.

WINDOWS UPDATE

Microsoft is constantly upgrading Windows 10 to be more secure and fix issues with specific hardware, so it's essential to keep it updated. Here we show you how.

USE WINDOWS UPDATE

Essential updates in Windows 10 are on by default. You can check your settings by searching 'update' in Cortana or by going to Settings > Update and Security > Windows Update. Choose Advanced options and check that it's set to Automatic.

Optional Updates

Some updates to Windows 10 aren't automatic, and these are generally ones that are unique to your system. When you load Windows Update it will tell you if there are any to be installed. You can then choose to Restart Now to have them installed.

Above: Microsoft often makes additions and improvements to Windows.

Pick a Time

It can be annoying to have to restart your PC when you're busy using it, so you can schedule your updates. You can choose a day and time from the drop-down menu. It will even suggest a time when you don't tend to use your PC. Since the Windows 10 Anniversary Update landed, it is now even easier to tell Windows 10 to update when it's convenient to you. Go to Settings > Update & Security > Windows Update and click on 'Change active hours'. From here you can tell Windows what times you use your PC, and Windows Update will avoid updating and restarting during those hours.

You also now have an option to log back in automatically when your PC reboots after an update. Go to 'Advanced Windows Update settings' and select 'Use my sign in info to automatically finish setting up my device after an update'.

Above: Make sure your PC doesn't restart while you're working on it by setting Active hours.

Uninstall Updates

If an update makes your PC worse, or there is a problem with it, you can uninstall updates after the event. You can view your update history by going to Advanced options and selecting View your update history. Tap or click Uninstall updates to find one you need to get rid of.

No More Updates

In the past if you reset or reinstalled Windows you would have to repeat every update, which could take hours, making it an unappealing thing to do. Luckily, that's no longer the case. The new PC Reset feature keeps the updates in place, so a quick refresh won't leave your Windows 10 PC unprotected.

Above: You can check what updates you've installed.

If you want to get the latest features for Windows 10, you can opt into preview builds in the Windows Update options menu. To take advantage, just click Get Started on the Get Insider builds screen and register for the latest improvements.

VIRUS PROTECTION

Windows 10 comes with its own antivirus program called Windows Defender. However, you can beef up your security with some free software. One of the best is called AVG Free.

INSTALL AVG

You can download AVG for free on the web, and it will add an extra layer of security to Windows 10. Here's how to get started.

Download

1. To download AVG Free just go to www.avg.com/gb-en/free-antivirus-protection

2. Choose to download the free product.

3. The download will be shown at the bottom of Microsoft Edge.

Above: You need good virus protection for your PC.

4. When completed, just choose Run.

5. In the installation screen press Continue and then make sure you check the box to get the free protection, not the paid-for product.

6. Click Install and allow the User Account control.

7. When the program opens, create an account by typing in an email address and password.

Protection

Click the Protection tab in AVG and you can get full options for your PC. There are five elements to AVG's protection and you can turn them all off by clicking the icons.

1. **Antivirus**: Real-time protection of your PC against viruses, spyware and trojans.

Above: AVG offers better protection than Windows Defender.

2. **Web**: The Linkscanner checks links you click on the web or social media and stops dangerous web pages from loading.

3. **Identity**: Checks that software on your PC isn't doing anything it shouldn't.

4. **Email**: Checks attachments for any harmful payloads.

Above: It also provides PC maintenance tools, too.

5. **Firewall**: Protects your PC from outside attacks – but this is the only element that requires a paid-for subscription.

Performance

Though not part of the standard AVG product, there's actually a separate tune-up tool for your PC. It's free, but will need to be installed. This will clean up free disk space, as well as extending your battery life. Just press the Get it free button to install.

ADVANCED WINDOWS 10 MAINTENANCE AND ADMINISTRATION

Windows 10 offers almost limitless control of your PC. While that means there are a lot of tools and utilities to learn, when things go wrong you have everything you need at your fingertips.

UNINSTALL WINDOWS PROGRAMS

Much of Windows maintenance is about keeping your installed programs in check. Read on for how to regain control of your PC.

The Difference Between Programs and Apps

Apps from the Windows Store are easy to get rid of; just right-click on any tile and then choose Uninstall. It's that simple. However, for deleting full-blown programs on your PC things are a little more difficult.

Above: You can remove apps quickly and easily.

Deleting Windows Programs

If you want to remove programs from Windows 10 just follow these steps.

1. Tap or click the Start menu and choose Settings.

2. Choose System.

3. Tap Apps & features.

4. Wait for the list to populate; it can take a few seconds.

5. Search for the app if you know which one you want to remove.

6. Check the amount of disk space used if you're looking to downsize.

7. Click any app then choose Uninstall to delete it from your system.

Above: Check if any apps are hogging space on your PC.

START-UP TOOL

By default a lot of Windows apps want to run as soon as your PC starts. But multiple apps vying for your PC's attention can make it slow.

In Windows 10 there's a handy tool that helps you keep start-up programs in check. Just follow the steps below to choose what you want to run.

1. On your keypad hit Ctrl + Alt + Delete or on a touch device tap and hold the Start menu and choose Task Manager.

Above: Too many apps starting with Windows can slow things down.

2. In the Task Manager menu choose the Start-up tab.

3. The list is populated with apps set to run when your Windows PC starts.

4. The impact column will show how much each program affects your start-up time.

5. Choose one that's not desired and just hit Disable from the list.

DEFRAGMENT AND OPTIMIZE DRIVES

The defrag tool (as it's known) in Windows 10 essentially gives your system a spring clean.

What Is Defragmenting?

Your PC will try to store all of the data from your Windows 10 system together, but as programs are added and removed, the order sometimes gets mixed up. That means older-style hard drives that write your data to a spinning disk have to work harder to retrieve the data. Defragmenting takes this mess of broken-up files and puts them back into a logical order.

Analyse Your Drives

Defragmenting can take a while, so luckily in Windows 10 you can analyse your disks to check whether you need to run the app. Just search for 'defrag' using Cortana and select Defragment and Optimize Drives. Choose a drive (generally use your C: drive) and then hit Analyse.

Above: Defragging your PC is like a hard drive spring clean.

Defragment

If you're registering a single-digit level of fragmentation then the gains will be minimal, but if your system is over 50% fragmented, your system is crying out for a spring clean. Just choose a drive and click Optimize to run the process.

Hot Tip
Defragging takes over your PC so get it scheduled. In the Defragment and Optimise Drives menu, click on Change Settings and choose a frequency.

DISK MANAGEMENT

The Disk Management tool is the gateway to serious control over your Windows 10 PC's hard drives.

What Can You Do In Disk Management?

You can check the health of your hard drive here and all the partitions on your PC. More importantly, you can start controlling how much space each one takes up.

Above: The Disk Management app enables you to resize and create new partitions on your hard drive.

Delete a Partition

If you feel that a secondary partition on your PC is taking up too much space, you can give the space it used up back to your C: drive. Click the partition and shrink the drive – the space made available will become unassigned in the bottom window. Then click the C: drive and choose Extend volume. Type in the amount of unassigned data and you've just made your hard drive bigger.

Create a Partition

Again, you will need to shrink a volume to create a partition, so follow the steps above. Then take the unassigned space and right-click. Choose New Simple Volume wizard, give it a new (unassigned) drive letter and you have a new drive.

Above: You can shrink large drives and offer the space to others.

TROUBLESHOOTING: WHAT TO DO WHEN THINGS GO WRONG

PC problems happen – it's a fact of life whatever type of system you have. Luckily in Windows 10 it's easier than ever to get things back on track.

Above: Check the Task Manager to see what's hogging your processor.

FIX A SLOW PC

A slow PC is one of the most common complaints, and also one of the most frustrating. But there are plenty of ways to get over the problem.

Find What's Hogging Your System

If your PC is going slow, it's important to find the root cause. First, wait for it to fully boot up, as that's a separate issue. If it's still crawling, then bring up the Task Manager by hitting Ctrl + Alt + Delete or right-clicking the Start menu.

In the Processes tab will be a list of all the apps that are running, and crucially the percentage of the CPU (processor) that each is taking up. If you see anything hogging your system, you can press End Task to kill it. You may consider removing the app for the future.

Trim Your Start-Up

If your PC takes an age to start, it's most likely due to too many programs trying to start at once. You can attack your start-up programs in the Task Manager. Turn to page 241 for a full guide.

Check Performance Monitor

The Performance Monitor app in Windows 10 enables you to collect performance reports and view them. Just search 'performance' in Cortana and open the app to determine how system changes such as ending processes or removing apps affect performance.

Above: Performance Monitor gives an overview of what your processor is up to.

Kill the Animations in Windows

All the whizz-bang animations in Windows can slow down systems that aren't up to the task, but happily they can be turned off. To disable animations, search for 'advanced system settings' in Cortana. Choose Performance and then check the box for Adjust for best performance. Windows will now be less slick but much faster.

Slow PC Checklist

- ○ Uninstall unwanted programs.

- ○ Close system tray programs.

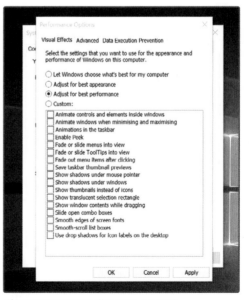

Above: Turn animations off to speed up your PC.

- Run a scan for malware.

- Download a program like CCleaner and sweep your registry.

- Reset your PC in Windows (see below).

FIX A PC THAT CRASHES

If your PC has suddenly started freezing, displaying a black screen, restarting or even suffering the dreaded blue screen of death, there are a range of tools you can turn to.

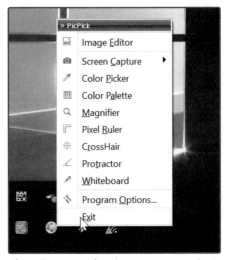

Above: Trim programs from the system tray to speed things up.

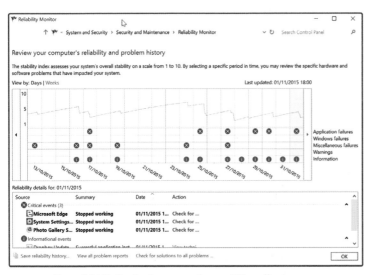

Above: Reliability Monitor shows any crashes your PC has suffered.

Check Reliability Monitor

Windows 10 has a tool called Reliability Monitor, which you can use to pinpoint the cause of crashes. If Windows has crashed or frozen, you'll see a red 'X' marked in the Windows failure column or the Application failure one. A Windows failure is a problem with the OS and the latter is with a specific app.

Read Reliability Monitor

If you can see your crash has been registered in Reliability Monitor as an application failure you can uninstall or update that specific feature. Windows 10 will also attempt to leave you useful information on events, such as the installation of new software or drivers, which can help pinpoint the root cause.

Above: Problem reports help Windows to identify problems and to notify you about solutions.

Perform a PC Reset

Many PC problems can be overcome using the Windows 10 reset feature. Just search 'recovery' using Cortana and then Reset this PC. Choose the option that keeps your files intact, and just resets Windows systems files.

Reset Your PC Without the Bloatware

Many PC manufacturers like to add apps and programs that you will never use. These are known as bloatware, and if you've spent time removing them, then performing a PC Reset is likely to restore them. Microsoft has made it easier to reset your PC to a clean Windows 10 installation without the bloatware. Open up Settings > Update & Security > Recovery and select 'Learn how to start afresh with a clean installation of Windows'. This takes you to a webpage where you can download a tool from Microsoft that will guide you through the process.

Above: Under 'More recovery options', you can get a fresh install of Windows 10 without all the annoying bloatware.

Run Windows Update

Crashes can be due to out-of-date drivers or software, which can be overcome by running Windows Update. Just search 'update' using Cortana and then open Windows Update.

FIX A PC THAT WON'T START

If your PC won't boot up and Windows 10 won't start, that can be one of the most difficult problems to solve. In that instance, follow the steps below.

Create and Use Recovery Media

If Windows 10 won't load then you will need a recovery disk. Your PC manufacturer will likely have supplied a recovery disk in the box, or you can make one in Windows 10.

If You Don't Have a Recovery Media and Your PC Won't Start

If you haven't got a recovery disk you can make one online. You'll need a PC or Mac (that starts) to access http://windows.microsoft.com/en-gb/windows-10/media-creation-tool-install.

How to Create a Recovery Disk in Windows 10

It's best to use a USB drive for creating a recovery disk, and as long as you have one over 16GB, you're good to go.

1. From the taskbar, search for Create a recovery drive then select it. You might be asked to enter your password.

2. When the tool opens, make sure Back up system files to the recovery drive is selected, then select Next.

3. Connect a USB drive to your PC, select it, then select Next > Create. The recovery disk will now be built.

← Recovery Drive

Select the USB flash drive

The drive must be able to hold at least 16 GB, and everything on the drive will be deleted.

Available drive(s)
   F:\ (FreeAgent GoFlex Drive)

Next   Cancel

Above: A recovery drive is worth having in case of a big PC problem.

Above: If it all goes wrong the advanced start can get things back on track.

How to Use a Recovery Disk in Windows 10

In the unfortunate event that you need your recovery disk, just plug it in and wait for it to boot. Search for 'recovery' in Cortana and choose the Advanced start. In the new menu choose Use a device. This will give you the option to recover your PC from the recovery drive.

Use a Recovery Disk on a PC That Won't Start

If your PC won't start then you will need to boot from the USB key. When your PC is off press and hold the F2 key and then turn it on. You will now enter the BIOS mode. Locate the boot tab and amend the order, so that USB booting is at the top of the list. Save and exit, and your PC should boot from the recovery key, enabling you to reinstall Windows files.

Hot Tip

Select Reset this PC then choose to keep or remove your files. You can also choose to have your PC wiped of everything, if you want to start completely afresh.

OTHER COMMON PC PROBLEMS SOLVED

There are plenty of niggling issues that can affect your PC. Here are some of the more common offenders and how to overcome them.

Devices Not Working

If your printer (or any device for that matter) stops working, then try these fixes.

Above: Windows 10 has a huge catalogue of devices it works with.

- Make sure that your printer is turned on and connected to your PC.

- If it still doesn't work, try running the printing troubleshooter.

- Try to find new drivers. First run Windows Update to look for optional upgrades. If that doesn't work open search 'devices and printers' in Cortana, select it from the list of results, and select your printer. Then select Remove device at the top of the screen.

- If Windows doesn't automatically find a new driver, look for one on the device manufacturer's website and follow their installation instructions.

Browser Is Slow

If your browser is slowing down, it might be due to extensions and plug-ins fighting for processing power. Depending on your browser go to the Settings menu and browser extensions, and remove plug-ins until you're back up to speed.

Pop-Up Ads on Your Desktop

If you're continually getting pop-ups or adverts on your PC's desktop and outside of traditional web ads, then it's likely your PC is infected with malware.

These programs can be notoriously difficult to get rid of, and you will need to scan your PC. It's vital that you use a respected name here, so first start with Windows Defender (see page 67 for how to scan). Alternatively, try AVG (http://free.avg.com) for a more powerful option.

Can't Connect the Wi-Fi

Make sure that the Wi-Fi is on. Go to Start > Settings > Network & Internet > WiFi. Choose the network and tap or click Connect.

If there's no connection, make sure that your router doesn't have any errors and that Wi-Fi is turned on. Often there is a function on the keyboard that acts as an on/off switch. Also, check that Flight mode is off in Settings > Network & Internet > Flight mode. Finally, ensure that you're close enough to your Wi-Fi router.

Above: Scan for viruses if your PC is slow.

Above: Wi-Fi troubleshooting can be done from the Settings menu.

Hot Tip
Never accept a pop-up advert to clear the malware from your PC. It's a common scam. Always choose reputable software.

USEFUL WEBSITES

www.askvg.com
A popular website that covers Windows tips, troubleshooting and customization.

www.computerhope.com/cleaning.htm
Tips and information on how to clean your computer without damaging it.

www.free.avg.com
The free version of the AVG antivirus and anti-spyware programs.

www.microsoft.com/en-gb/software-download/windows10ISO
Get Windows 10 installed on your computer.

www.microsoft.com/en-gb/windows
Learn about Windows 10, the latest devices, apps and games or find support.

www.microsoft.com/en-gb/windows/apps-and-games
The web based app store for Windows 10.

www.nidirect.gov.uk/choosing-a-computer
Advice on the best type of computer to choose for your needs, with links to other computer-related basics.

www.pcadvisor.co.uk
Great advice on all things PC: device reviews, articles, forums and more.

www.recyclenow.com
Includes what to do with your computer once you're done using it – you don't want to just throw it in the bin.

http://store.steampowered.com
A huge catalogue of the greatest video games, which can be downloaded to your Windows 10 PC for the best in gaming entertainment.

www.strongpasswordgenerator.com
A guide to choosing a good password.

www.windowsforum.com
Information on how to deal with many common issues and questions about Windows.

http://windows.microsoft.com/en-us/windows/preview-supported-phones
A list of the devices on which you can run Windows 10.

https://windows.microsoft.com/en-gb/windows-10/media-creation-tool-install
A guide to reinstalling Windows from another computer if your computer won't start.

www.xbox.com/en-US/windows-10
Take gaming to the next level by connecting your Xbox with your Windows 10 PC.

FURTHER READING

Amobi, Onuora, *Inside Windows 10: An Early Look at Microsoft's Newest Operating System*, Onuora Amobi, 2015

Bott, Ed, *Introducing Windows 10 for IT Professionals, Preview Edition*, Microsoft Press, 2015

Gleam, Jacob, *Windows 10: A Beginner's Guide*, CreateSpace Independent Publishing Platform, 2015

Halsey Mike, *Windows 10 Primer*, Apress, 2015

Hart, Brian, *Windows 10: The Ultimate User Guide for Beginners*, CreateSpace Independent Publishing Platform, 2015

Knittel, Brian & McFedries, Paul, *Windows 10 In Depth*, QUE, 2015

Muir Boysen, Nancy, *Windows 10 Plain & Simple*, Microsoft Press, 2015

Pogue, David, *Windows 10: The Missing Manual*, O'Reilly Media, 2015

Price, Michael, *Windows 10 for Seniors*, In Easy Steps Ltd, 2015

Rathbone, Andy, *Windows 10 for Dummies*, John Wiley & Sons, 2015

Soper, Mark Edward, *Easy Windows 10*, QUE, 2015

Stanek, William, *Windows 10: The Personal Trainer*, CreateSpace Independent Publishing Platform, 2015

Tidrow, Rob, & Boyce, Jim & Shapiro, Jeffrey R., *Windows 10 Bible*, Wiley, 2015

Vandome, Nick, *Get Going with Windows 10*, In Easy Steps Ltd, 2015

Wilson, Kevin, *Computer Training: Windows 10*, Elluminet Press, 2015

INDEX